AF076887

FINANCE ESSENTIALS FOR START-UP ENTREPRENEURS

PRADEEP SWAMINATHAN
PROF. TRILOCHAN SASTRY

© **Professor Trilochan Sastry and Pradeep Swaminathan 2022**

All rights reserved

All rights reserved by author. No part of this publication may be reproduced, stored in a retrieval system or transmitted in any form or by any means, electronic, mechanical, photocopying, recording or otherwise, without the prior permission of the author.

Although every precaution has been taken to verify the accuracy of the information contained herein, the author and publisher assume no responsibility for any errors or omissions. No liability is assumed for damages that may result from the use of information contained within.

First Published in April 2022

ISBN: 978-93-5611-361-9

BLUEROSE PUBLISHERS

www.bluerosepublishers.com
info@bluerosepublishers.com
+91 8882 898 898

Cover Design:
Jaya P Swaminathan

Typographic Design:
Rohit

Editor:
Jaya P Swaminathan

Illustrator:
S R Krishnan

Distributed by: BlueRose, Amazon, Flipkart

This book is dedicated to Prof. Janak Raj Mongia of Sriram College of Commerce, who introduced me to the fundamentals of accounts and finance.

-- Pradeep Swaminathan

Authors' Note

This book is not intended to be part of any formal course but rather a handbook to manage the finances of a business. However, if you understand the concepts enunciated in this book, it will help you do well in any course on finance. This book has been written primarily for entrepreneurs and non-finance executives.

Finance and Accounts is a vast subject and a formal study could take some years. What we have tried to do in this book is to simplify those topics which are very essential and basic in the day-to-day running of a business. If you go through these pages and try to grasp these basic principles, there is every chance that you can master the basics of finance to run your business.

You must be familiar with the Pareto principle. In most cases eighty percent of the effect comes from twenty percent of the causes. Examples: twenty percent of your customers give eighty percent of the revenue, twenty percent of the stock items are eighty percent of your inventory in value, twenty percent of the people in your life give you eighty percent of your happiness. Successful people devote most of their attention to this twenty percent. Similarly, in running a business, twenty percent of the theories of finance and accounts are important for running eighty percent of your business. It is this twenty percent that we have tried to simplify and put across to you in this book, both in text and in a presentation.

The presentation that follows the main text, was given to a batch of entrepreneurs who had enrolled for a popular programme designed by IIM Bangalore for founders of new start-ups. The presentation was very well received by the students and so has been made part of this book.

Today, as individuals we drive cars, use computers and browse the net. It is not necessary that we should know everything about cars, computers and the net to be good users. Similarly, one need not be a chartered accountant or a finance person to know the financial aspects of a business. Just as the driver of a car knows how to steer, change gears, use the accelerator and brake, refer to the panels and modify the speed of the car depending on the environment; as a business person, you should know how to financially steer your business. This book tells you just that and in very simple terms.

We are grateful to Jaya Swaminathan for editing this book and her inputs in making it simpler to understand.

Lastly, all sale proceeds and royalties that will be received from the first edition of this book will go to the Centre for Collective Development, an NGO that facilitates poor farmers to become economically independent and help them escape the vicious cycle of money lenders and debt traps. You will have the satisfaction of knowing that your money has not only been spent to improve your grasp of finance but also to help impoverished farmers in India.

PRADEEP SWAMINATHAN and

PROFESSOR TRILOCHAN SASTRY

01/03/ 2022

BANGALORE, INDIA

Contents

Introduction To Accounts 1
Capital Versus Revenue 3
Fixed Cost Versus Variable Cost 9
Cost-Benefit Analysis... 15
Marginal Costing.. 21
Cost Reduction – How And Where To Reduce Costs 30
Balance Sheet – What Does It Convey?................................. 36
The Effect Of An Incomplete Cash Cycle............................. 44
Balance Sheet Of A Corporate 46
Cash Flows 54
Discounted Cash Flows 63
Amortization Of Costs.. 70
Accounting Standards.. 71
Selling On Credit – Pitfalls 72
Financing The Business: Equity And Debt 76
Valuations.. 83
Presentation to Start-Up Entrepreneurs at IIM Bangalore.... 89

Introduction To Accounts

Accounts is the language of business and commerce. As in everything else, the bigger the business, the more complex the accounts get. Money and accounts go hand in hand. Anything that is scarce must be monitored. For some reason, ever since man invented money, it has been scarce, and it has had to be accounted for. We all have been accountants in one way or the other. Till we started earning, we got money from our parents. Yes, we had mentally mapped what money we had and how we could spend it – movies, a lunch out, maybe a bar of chocolate, etc. Once we started earning, we again took the role of an accountant. This is roughly our income, and this is what our expenditure should be; rent for the house or EMI for the house, children's fees, clothes, food, etc. If you see the movement from pocket money to salary, our accounts became that much more complex. The principles of accounts remain the same whether you are an individual, a start-up, an established corporate or a nation. When you are dealing with someone else's money, ethics demand that you give a perfect account of what you have spent. Your mother would probably be the first accountant you came across. She may not have known the intricacies of double entry book-keeping and her ledger would have been the humble diary of a year back, but she nevertheless kept track of every bit of money that was spent.

The aim of this book is not to teach you to become an accountant but open a window that will help you analyse the accounts and help you to grasp the main principles. This is especially relevant when you are managing your own enterprise or start-up.

The major concepts that will be touched on are:

Capital versus Revenue – What goes to the Profit and Loss Account and why, what goes to the Balance Sheet and why.

Fixed Cost versus Variable Cost – What is the difference and why it is important.

Principles of Contribution and Marginal Costing.

Cost Reduction – How and where to reduce costs.

Balance Sheet – What it conveys.

Cash Flow Statements – Importance.

Amortization of costs – What this means and how it affects the profits of an organization.

Accounting Standards – What are they and how it might affect you.

Selling on Credit – Pitfalls.

Borrowing – The risk when you take debt.

Valuations.

Important points to be conveyed while requesting for funds.

Once again it is reiterated that the purpose is not to make you an accountant, but someone who can read accounts and understand what the accounts are trying to tell you. The aim is to help people in start-ups so that they can have a better grasp of the concepts. Each concept will be corelated to issues of a start-up.

Let us now go on to the first concept.

Capital Versus Revenue

- Shorn of all jargon, this concept will try to explain what expenditure should go to calculating profit and what should not. That expenditure and income which is used to calculate the profit or loss, is called revenue and that which is not, is called capital.

- From the above point we have two types of expenditure, capital – that expenditure which is not utilised for calculating the Profit and Loss and revenue – which is used for calculating the Profit and Loss.

- Why is this important? If we do not know the difference and use all expenditure to calculate the profit or loss, we will not be informing ourselves and the investors correctly regarding the profit or the loss.

- Generally capital expenditure involves that expenditure, the benefit of which lasts over a period of time. Let us take the example of a television set. When we buy a television set, we expect it to work for several years. When we buy a house, we expect that it should last us for our lifetime. Similarly, when we buy a car, we expect that it will last us for ten years.

- In the above examples, what is that we see in common? The benefit of the expenditure stretches over a few years, ranging from five to fifty plus years. Also, the money involved is on the higher side. When we buy a fountain pen, we expect it also to last several years. I know of some friends and family members who have kept their fountain pens going for twenty years and will not dream of using another pen to do something important. Here since the amount involved is not very high, it is fully charged to Profit and Loss account and used for calculating the profit.

- As opposed to capital expenditure, the benefit of revenue expenditure does not last over several years. It may last a month or a year. Certainly not over several years. For example, the monthly wages you pay your maid servant to clean your house and utensils. Once you pay her for the month and even if you have closed your house for twenty days, you have to pay her again. The wages that you pay your maid is revenue expenditure. Another example of revenue expenditure is rent. The rent that you pay for your flat entitles you to live in that flat for the month. Come next month and again you have to pay the rent. The vegetables, the groceries, the electricity, the water, the maintenance charges are all expenditure related to the month. These are all revenue expenditure.

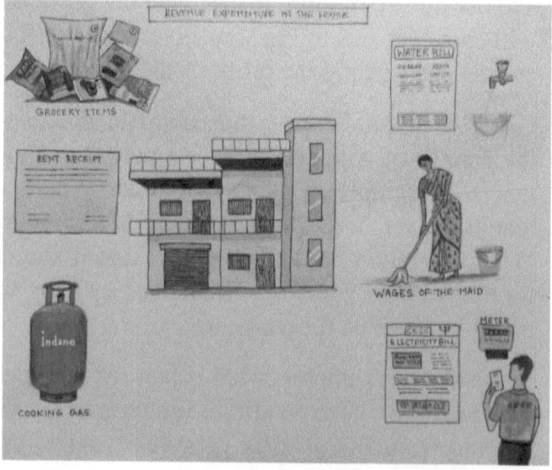

- Let us now say, you buy a dishwasher that costs you ₹1,20,000. This dishwasher will last you for five years. Is it capital or revenue? From what little we have understood, it is capital. After five years the dishwasher will conk out and you have to replace it with a new one. A prudent accountant will calculate the expenditure per year. This will come to ₹24,000 (1,20,000/5). He will charge ₹24,000 each year to the profit and loss account. This is the concept of depreciation. If you calculate the monthly depreciation, it will be ₹2,000 (24,000/12). This is one way of calculating depreciation. There are other methods also. The actual method of calculating depreciation depends on the laws and rules then in place.

- You will see that this monthly depreciation is similar to the wages that you pay your maid servant for washing the dishes. If the environment where you live has a high wage structure (you have to pay the maid more than ₹2000), it does not make sense for you to hire a maid but buy a dishwasher and if it is an environment where you have a low wage structure, it makes sense to hire a maid.

- To conclude: expenditure, the benefit of which will be enjoyed over several years is capital; expenditure, the benefit of which is enjoyed in the current year is revenue. The yearly depreciation of a capital asset is also charged to the Profit and Loss account (revenue).

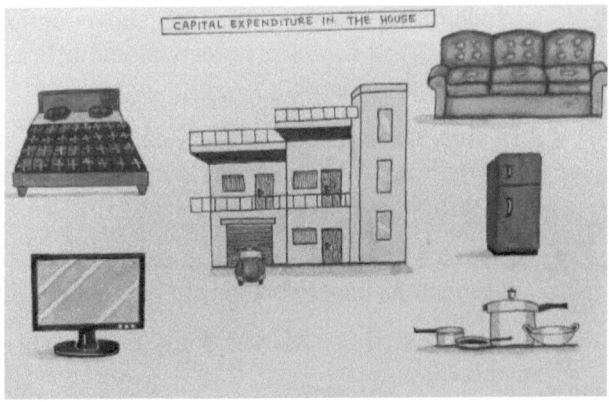

In the next few pages, we will see that the various expenditures a start-up has at the beginning.

What Are The Capital And Revenue Expenses At The Beginning Of A Start-up?

1. You will have to have a place from which you and your team will operate. It could be your father's garage, it could be your study, or it could be a 'plug and play', a shared workspace or individual space. Here, you will have to do a cost-benefit analysis between buying, renting, or trying to get this free. We all dream of the big bucks. Do not start spending big before you start earning big. Do not be penny wise pound foolish; do not compromise on quality but try to get value for your money.

   - Father's garage – free of cost
   - Friend's study – free of cost
   - Renting office space in the centre of the city – revenue expenditure – very costly. Unless you get a tangible benefit do not do this.
   - Renting space in the outskirts of the city – revenue expenditure, cheaper than the above option and maybe if you combine residential and office space, can be a good option.
   - Buying space in the outskirts of the city – capital expenditure – huge cash outflow at the beginning of the project. Is it worth it?
   - Shared workspace – revenue expenditure – much cheaper than buying but may have other restrictions.

2. Feasibility study or Market Study before you start a business.
   - Such expenditure is normally capital in nature.

3. Purchase of computers, software and internet connection.
   - Try to purchase second-hand computers initially. If you and your team have their own laptops, then perhaps, you do not need to buy. As your business grows you can upgrade.
   - Computer – capital expenditure.
   - Software – depending on the type can be capital or revenue, example software you pay for one time but use for many years will be capital, the licence fee you pay every year will be revenue expenditure.
   - Internet connection will be revenue expenditure.
   - Mobile Phone – capital expenditure – keep it functional, avoid frills.
   - Services provider – revenue expenditure.
4. Travel Expenditure – revenue – use online meetings to avoid this.
5. Furniture – capital expenditure – try to get free or second-hand furniture.
6. Machinery – purchase this and it is capital expenditure but if you rent it, the expenditure will be revenue.
7. Local travel – purchasing a car – capital expenditure, renting transport – revenue expenditure.

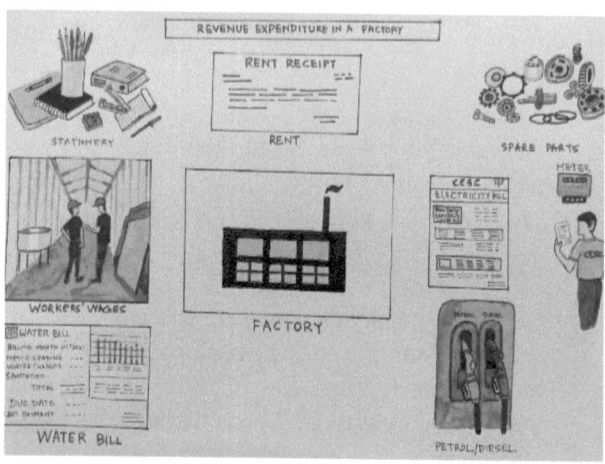

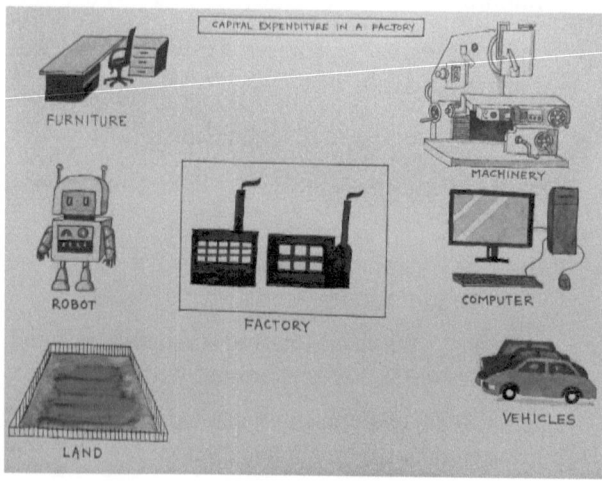

The above illustrates what constitutes capital and what constitutes revenue. A simple thumb rule to follow, keep capital expenditure to a minimum in your early days. If you have doubts do a cost-benefit exercise, which will be explained later in this book.

Fixed Cost Versus Variable Cost

When you start your business, you will realise that there are costs that are to be incurred irrespective of whether you produce and sell or not. Let us go to the examples we are all best familiar with, our house. Your family pays monthly rent for the house. This is fixed. Let us assume it is a two-bedroom house. The rent remains fixed whether you stay there or not. The family takes time off and goes to Goa for a holiday. There you stay in a hotel. That cost varies on the number of days you stay at the hotel. The more days you stay, the more you pay. The fewer days you stay, the less you pay. As far as your house rent is concerned, it does not matter whether you stay in the house or not. You have to pay rent. Rent is a fixed cost to your family but the hotel cost is variable. The food you eat at home is variable. So is the electricity. The more days you stay at home, the more electricity you consume. Let us now take the hotel example again. At the hotel, irrespective of how long you use the air conditioner, you do not pay for the electricity. Unlike in the house, the electricity cost does not change. We have two situations; the house rent is fixed, and the hotel rent is variable. Similarly, the electricity cost in your house is variable but, in the hotel, it is fixed. So, we come to this very important conclusion that it is not the nature of the cost that makes it fixed or variable but the agreement you enter as to how you pay it that makes it fixed or variable. In most hotels, when you pay for your room rent, breakfast is included. Hence, the food, at least as far as breakfast is concerned, is fixed for you. At home for your family, the rent is fixed, the electricity is variable, and the food is variable. At the hotel, the rent is variable, the electricity is fixed and the food as far as breakfast is concerned, is fixed. You eat at the hotel or you do not, you use the air-conditioner or not, you do not have to incur any extra expenditure, so it is fixed. If you have breakfast elsewhere you have to pay. For the hotel owner on the other hand electricity and breakfast is variable. The hotel owner pays for the electricity depending on the number of units you have consumed or for eggs depending on the number of eggs you have eaten. Assuming for a minute he is paying rent to the owner of the building, the rent is fixed. So, for you the rent is variable, and breakfast and electricity are fixed and for the hotelier, the rent he pays is fixed and the electricity and food are variable.

What is so important about the cost being fixed or variable? Is it just some classification accountants have come with?

You are now paying an annual rent of ₹1,00,000 for a building in which you manufacture sensors. Let us say the full annual capacity is 1,00,000 sensors. If you manufacture 1,00,000 sensors, the cost is ₹1 per sensor (₹1,00,000/1,00,0000). If you manufacture 50,000 sensors, the cost is ₹2 per sensor. But if you manufacture 20,000 sensors, the cost per sensor is ₹5 (₹1,00,000/20,000). So, when the cost is fixed and the output is low, the cost per unit increases. This means that in case your start-up is not able to market its products well in the initial period, you will be incurring high costs for being idle.

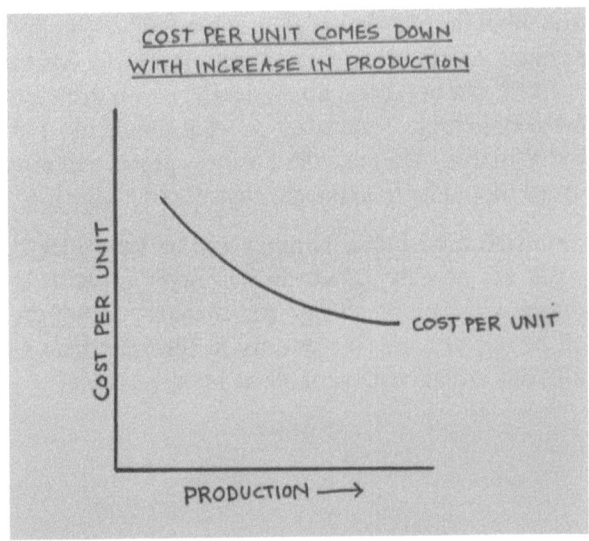

In the example of the sensor, you buy material for sensors. Let us say, a small chip. The chips you will buy depend on the number you plan to manufacture. If you plan to manufacture 10,000 sensors you will buy only 10,000 chips. So, your variable cost (raw material) per sensor does not change with production.

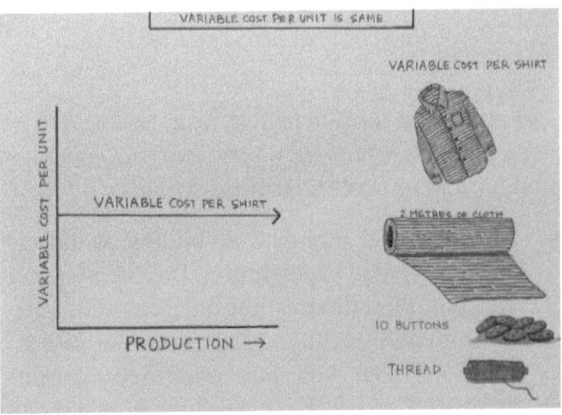

To summarise what we have clarified so far, a fixed cost does not change with your activity level whereas your variable cost does. The more the activity level, the cheaper per unit the fixed cost becomes and the less your activity level, the costlier per unit the fixed cost becomes. So, logically, if you think early on in your business there is uncertainty, what should most of your costs be? Variable. Also, as your business grows and prospers, the attempt should be to make the costs fixed.

When you start a business, earnings will be very uncertain. If your costs are mainly fixed, as has been explained, your expenditure will have to be met and if things do not go well, you will be out of cash. We will try to illustrate here how to make all your initial costs variable as far as possible.

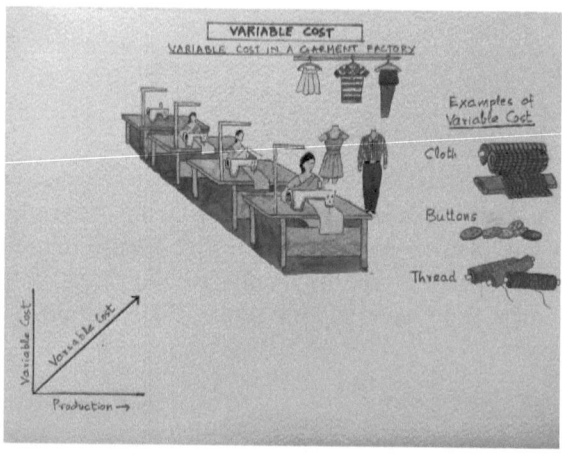

> You now want a place to start your business. From that place you either provide a service or you manufacture a product. Let us take the various options.

- Buy land and fabricate a building at the outskirts. This is capital expenditure. The advantage is after you buy this, there is not much expenditure. But it will involve a huge cash outflow. What is the solution? Can you buy unutilised capacity in a factory? You achieve everything with a much lower cash flow.

- Take a 'Pay as you use' contract. Then you can avoid a huge cash flow and make your costs linked to production. In effect, these costs are variable.

- Rent a premises. You will have a much lower cash outflow as above. The disadvantage is that it is a fixed cost. Whether you manufacture or not, your service generates a cash flow or not, you will pay rent. Maybe because of your business model, you need an outlet in the centre of the city. By all means, rent a place. Only accept that this is a fixed cost, and you will have to pay the rent irrespective of whether you get any income or not.

- Shared office space. It is much cheaper to rent a desk or a couple of desks. Again, like in the example above, similar to renting capacity in a factory, you can rent a couple of desks for those people who have to be visible, the back office can work from a garage or a place in the outskirts or even from their homes.

- Use your uncle or father's garage. If you can get it free, that may be the best solution.

➢ Your business makes you move around the city. Let us see the various options.

- Buy a car and hire a driver. Huge cash outflow. Regular bills to pay car insurance, salary of driver. Lot of costs are fixed and even if you don't use the car, you will have to pay fixed costs.

- Use a car rental service. You have to pay only when you make a trip, so it is a variable cost. It is best to do a cost-benefit analysis. This is illustrated at the end of this chapter.

➢ You require software to run your business

- If possible, look at open-source software.

➤ One of the most important requisites of any business will be people. Remember the wage cost is always fixed. Whether your business makes money or not, the wages you pay are fixed. How does one make this variable without it adversely impacting your business or exploiting your team?

- Make the wages part fixed, part variable and part based on profits.

- Have people working on hourly basis: People who have recently retired – they bring with them the wealth of experience and for a majority of them, money is not a criterion but they will jump at the prospect of doing something challenging. Consider employing qualified individuals for whom working from home is a necessity – those having an infant at home or elderly parents to be looked after.

- Outsourcing: use the services of a firm on an hourly basis to do some jobs. Examples of jobs that could be outsourced are accounting, tax, security, services like electricity, housekeeping etc.

Cost-Benefit Analysis

Let us take a couple of simple examples to understand how to do a cost-benefit analysis. Once we are clear with these simple examples, we will try to move to more complicated ones.

Example 1: Buying a washing machine versus hiring a maid to wash the clothes versus using a laundromat.

Step 1 Clearly enunciate the option

Buying A Washing Machine

Step 2

What are various expenditures involved with the machine?

- Capital cost (to buy the machine) ₹20,000
- Annual electricity cost ₹3000
- Lifetime maintenance cost ₹4000
- Cost of detergent annually 25 kgs @ ₹120/kg

Step 3

Annualise this cost. How do we make this cost yearly?

- The cost to buy the machine is ₹20,000. The machine lasts ten years. Spread out over ten years, the annual cost is ₹2000
- The annual electricity cost is ₹3000. No further action required.
- Maintenance cost is ₹4000 over lifetime. Annual cost is ₹400
- Detergent cost is ₹3000
- The total annual cost is ₹12000

Now we repeat the above steps for a maid servant

Step 1

Hiring A Maid

Step 2

Expenditure involved in hiring a maid

- Salary for washing clothes is ₹600 per month
- Diwali and festival tips ₹2000 per year
- Requests to pay the maid's kids' fees ₹1000 per year
- Tea and biscuits for the maid ₹100 per month
- Cost of detergents annually is 30 kgs @ ₹120/kg (assuming she will use more)

Step 3

Annualise the costs

- Salary ₹7200
- Other costs involving the maid ₹3000
- Tea and biscuits ₹1200
- Detergents ₹3600
- Total costs ₹15000

Now we repeat the steps for using a laundromat near your house

Step 1

Using A Laundromat

Step 2

The laundromat charges are as follows

- Vest ₹2 per piece
- Brief ₹2 per piece
- Pyjama ₹3 per piece
- Kurta or T-shirt ₹3 per piece
- Shirt or Top ₹4 per piece
- Trouser ₹5 per piece

Step 3

- You will put for wash 365 pieces of underclothes. (365 x 2) + (365 x 2) = ₹1460.
- You wash your pyjamas and t-shirts on alternate day so 183 x 3 plus 183 x 3 = ₹1098.
- Shirts 365 x 4 = ₹1460
- Trousers 183 x 5 = ₹915
- Total annual cost is ₹4933
- Since the laundromat is near your house, there is no transport cost.

The laundromat wins hands down.

Example 2: Buying a car versus hiring a car

Step 1

Buying A Car

Step 2

What are the costs that relate to buying and using a car?

- Capital Cost ₹8,00,000

- Driver's salary ₹10,000 per month
- Lifetime maintenance over the useful life ₹4,00,000
- Insurance and road tax ₹20,000 per annum
- Petrol at the cost of ₹73 per litre

Step 3

We now have to annualise the costs of the car

- Capital Cost = ₹8,00,000
- Life in years = 10
- Sale value at end of 10 years = ₹1,00,000
- Cost to owner = ₹7,00,000

Annual cost = ₹70,000

- Monthly salary of driver = ₹10,000
- Annual salary = ₹1,20,000
- Medical, Bonus etc = ₹20,000

Annual Cost = ₹1,40,000

- Lifetime maintenance = ₹4,00,000;

Annual Cost = ₹40,000

Insurance and Road Tax = ₹20,000 per annum

The fixed cost = ₹2,70,000 (whether you drive a single km or not)

In a year, the car is driven 1,00,000 km

This car gives a mileage of 10km per litre of petrol. So, you will buy 10,000 litres

The variable cost will be ₹7,30,000 @ ₹73/l

Annual cost of having your own car is ₹10,00,000

Step 1

Hiring A Car

Step 2

What are the costs that relate to hiring a car?

The cost of hiring a car is ₹14 per km

Step 3

In a year, the car is used for 1,00,000 km

Annual cost of hiring a car is ₹14,00,000

1. Looking at it on a purely cost basis, it makes sense to buy your car, if you are travelling 1,00,000 km in an annum
2. If you are travelling 50,000 km in an annum, does it make economic sense to buy a car?
   - Owning a car:

     Fixed cost will not change = ₹2,70,000

     Variable cost: This car gives a mileage of 10km per litre of petrol. So, you will buy 5,000 litres

     ₹73 x 5,000 = ₹3,65,000

     Total = ₹6,35,000
   - Annual cost of hiring a car = ₹7,00,000
   - It can be clearly seen that as the kilometres reduce, the cost of hiring a car becomes more economical. This is because of the role of fixed costs.

When does it break even?

The equation below will answer that question

Since we get 10 km/l of petrol,

2,70,000 + (73 ÷ 10) x number of km = 14 x number of km

2,70,000 = 6.7 x number of km

number of km = 40,298

If you are travelling less than this, it makes sense to hire a car; more than this, it makes sense to buy a car.

Following this simple method, a quick decision can be taken regarding buying or hiring.

Marginal Costing

Marginal costing helps us to make decisions regarding how much to produce and at what price we should sell. This is a very important concept and sometimes start-ups ignore it and end up in loss. Why are we making a loss? How can we avoid making a loss? What quantities should we sell? After understanding this concept, we will work out some basic illustrations.

As you may recall, selling price is the price we charge to the customer for which he pays us money. Please note, it is not the price on the brochure or price-tag. In some cases, the list price and the selling price can be the same. Where there is a discount over the list price, the selling price will be the list price after the discount. Any commissions paid to selling agents should also be deducted. So, the selling price is the actual price received by the business. Where there are products to be sold, it is the selling price per product. Where it is a service, it is the selling price per hour, per day, per month or per year.

Marginal cost is the variable cost of a product or a service. We have discussed the concept of fixed and variable cost in the previous chapter. Fixed cost does not change with the output of an organization whereas variable cost varies with the output. Please see the illustration below where all these terms are hopefully made clear.

Illustration

We have set up a small factory where Pashmina shawls are made. Four craftsmen have been employed and they are paid based on their output. For each shawl they are given ₹10,000. The material for the shawl including the thread and other accessories is ₹15,000 per shawl. As part of the contract with the workers, the workers are provided with accommodation and food. Part of the space where they are accommodated is utilised exclusively as a shop floor for manufacture of the shawls. The rent for their accommodation and shop floor comes to ₹60,000 per month. The four workers are able to manufacture twenty shawls per month. Depending on the month, the number of shawls sold vary along with the price. You have a discussion with your accountant regarding each month. The best period is the quarter October to December. You get a price of ₹40,000 per shawl. You can sell 60 shawls. The next best season is January to March. The price falls to ₹35,000 per shawl but you are able to sell 60. The season April to June is worst. You can sell only 40 shawls at ₹20,000 per shawl. The season July to August is marginally better. You can sell 40 shawls at ₹27,000 per shawl. Your accountant gives you the following calculations.

We will evaluate these calculations together.

Season 1

Income

60 shawls at ₹40,000 per shawl = ₹24,00,000

Marginal or Variable cost

Per shawl Labour = ₹10,000

  Material = ₹15,000

  Total = ₹25,000

Number of shawls made = 60

Variable cost of 60 shawls = ₹15,00,000

Contribution = ₹9,00,000

Note: Contribution is not your profit. We have yet to deduct the fixed costs. Contribution is what you get when you deduct variable cost from selling price.

Fixed Cost is ₹60,000 per month. So, the fixed cost for the quarter is ₹1,80,000.

Profit = Contribution − Fixed Cost

= ₹9,00,000 − ₹1,80,000

= ₹7,20,000

When the organization does well, there is no necessity for deep analysis.

Season 2

Income

60 shawls at ₹35,000 per shawl = ₹21,00,000

Marginal or Variable cost

Per shawl Labour = ₹10,000

Material = ₹15,000

Total = ₹25,000

Number of shawls made = 60

Variable cost of 60 shawls = ₹15,00,000

Contribution = ₹6,00,000

Note: Contribution is not your profit. We have yet to deduct the fixed costs. Contribution is what you get when you deduct variable cost from selling price.

Fixed Cost is ₹60,000 per month. So, the fixed cost for the quarter is ₹1,80,000.

Profit = Contribution − Fixed Cost

= ₹6,00,000 − ₹1,80,000

= ₹4,20,000

The organization is still doing well, there is no necessity for deep analysis.

Season 3

Income

40 shawls at ₹20,000 per shawl = ₹8,00,000

Marginal or Variable cost

Per shawl Labour   = ₹10,000

         Material = ₹15,000

         Total   = ₹25,000

Number of shawls made = 40

Variable cost of 40 shawls = ₹10,00,000

Contribution = – ₹2,00,000

Note: Contribution is not your profit. We have yet to deduct the fixed costs. Contribution is what you get when you deduct variable cost from selling price.

Fixed Cost is ₹60,000 per month. So, the fixed cost for the quarter is ₹1,80,000.

Profit = Contribution – Fixed Cost

      = – ₹2,00,000 – ₹1,80,000

      = – ₹3,80,000

The organization is in loss, there is now a necessity for deep analysis.

Issues to consider:

- You cannot change the market. So, your income is fixed
- You are not even able to cover your variable costs. It does not help. You will be losing money if you continue to make shawls.
- Speak to your workers. Tell them times are bad. If they are ready to cut their labour costs to ₹7,000, you can keep them. If they are unwilling to do so, you have to tell

them that they will have to look for employment elsewhere.

- Similarly, you will have to negotiate with your suppliers. Tell them that you have dropped prices and demand a 20% discount. Let us say they agree. For them also it is a matter of survival.

So now let us recalculate the scenario.

Income

40 shawls at ₹20,000 per shawl = ₹8,00,000

Marginal or Variable cost

Per shawl Labour   = ₹7,000
          Material = ₹12,000
          Total   = ₹19,000

Number of shawls made = 40

Variable cost of 40 shawls = ₹7,60,000

Contribution = ₹40,000

Note: Contribution is not your profit. We have yet to deduct the fixed costs. Contribution is what you get when you deduct variable cost from selling price.

Fixed Cost is ₹60,000 per month. So, the fixed cost for the quarter is ₹1,80,000/

Profit = Contribution – Fixed Cost

   = ₹40,000 – ₹1,80,000

   = – ₹1,40,000

Now some tough decisions must be taken. Should you stop the business? Consequences are – restarting is tough, your employees may be poached, the costs may go up if you restart. If you retain the premises, you lose ₹1,80,000. If you stop work, and restart in the good season, you will have to incur fixed cost of ₹1,80,000 anyway. However, if you produce shawls, you will get ₹40,000. You make the choice. If you continue your business, the loss is less. All this analysis is possible because we have distinguished between fixed and variable cost.

Season 4

Income

40 shawls at ₹27,000 per shawl = ₹10,80,000

Marginal or Variable cost

Per shawl Labour   = ₹10,000

          Material = ₹15,000

          Total   = ₹25,000

Number of shawls made = 40

Variable cost of 40 shawls = ₹10,00,000

Contribution = ₹80,000

Note: Contribution is not your profit. We have yet to deduct the fixed costs. Contribution is what you get when you deduct variable cost from selling price.

Fixed Cost is ₹60,000 per month. So, the fixed cost for the quarter is ₹1,80,000

Profit = Contribution – Fixed Cost

      = ₹80,000 – ₹1,80,000

      = – ₹1,00,000

The organization is at a loss, there is now a necessity for deep analysis.

This has been explained in the above scenario. You will have to negotiate costs downwards once again.

Broadly we have had three scenarios.

Scenario 1: The business makes a profit

Scenario 2: The business is not able to recover its variable costs. This is a dangerous situation and it really does not make sense in running the business on a long term. Unless the issue of at least covering your variable cost is addressed, it does not make sense in continuing with this business.

Scenario 3: You have covered your variable cost but not your fixed cost. It does make sense to continue this business and in the long run with some sound strategies in place to reduce costs, the business should thrive.

Break Even point

Contribution – Fixed Cost = Profit

We have understood this equation above.

Breakeven point is that level where Profit is zero i.e., where your contribution is equal to fixed cost. Above breakeven point, we make profit and below that, we make a loss.

Illustration

In the above example, let us try to capture the breakeven point for a quarter

Contribution = Fixed Cost

Fixed Cost for the quarter is ₹1,80,000

Contribution per shawl is ₹15,000

With the price remaining fixed as in the top two seasons

So, ₹15,000 x number of shawls = ₹1,80,000

Number of shawls = 12

So above 12 shawls we make a profit and below 12 we make a loss.

Using this simple tool, we get an idea of how much we should sell and at what price. It helps in negotiations and in strategies to reduce cost.

In the same example your distributor tells you that if you reduce the price to ₹10,000 per shawl, he will be able to sell a greater number of shawls. What will be the breakeven number?

₹10,000 x number of shawls = ₹1,80,000

The answer obviously is 18 shawls.

Let us summarize the above discussions in the form of graphs.

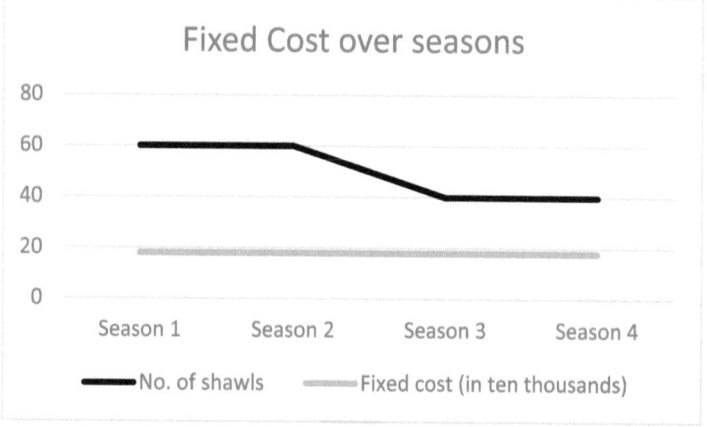

Fixed cost does not change with increase or decrease in output of the product.

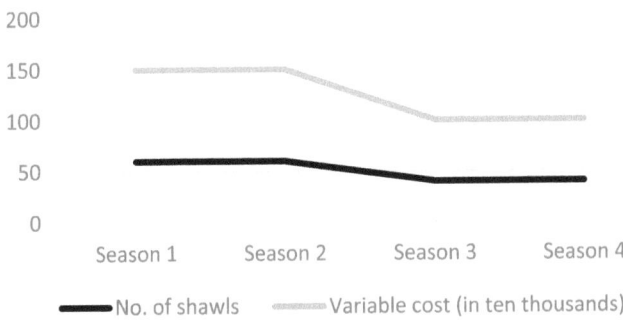

Variable cost changes with increase or decrease in output of the product. It is directly proportional to the output: as output decreases, variable cost decreases; as output increases, variable cost increases.

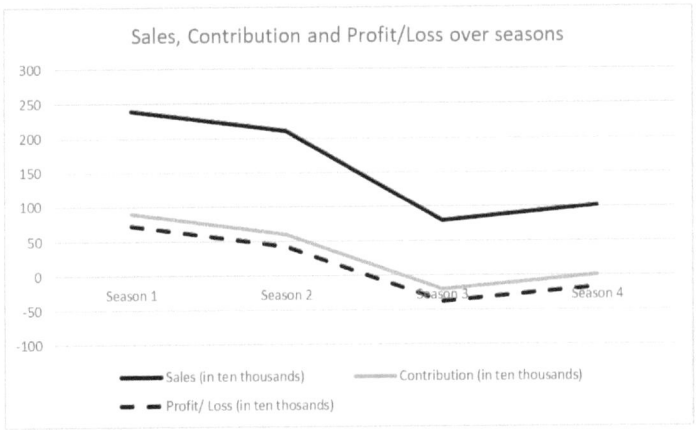

Contribution changes with increase or decrease in sales. As sales decreases, contribution decreases; as sales increases, contribution increases. Profit also increases or decreases with increase or decrease in sales. The gap between contribution and profit is always the same as it is equal to the fixed cost.

Cost Reduction – How And Where To Reduce Costs

Penny wise, pound foolish. This totally applies to cost reduction and when you apply it in your personal or professional life, it makes total sense.

Simple example: You buy a sneaker that costs ₹200 which lasts you for two months. Your neighbour buys a sneaker that costs ₹1200 which lasts him two years. The shoe you purchased cost you ₹100 per month and the shoe your neighbour purchased cost him ₹50 per month. Prima facie, your neighbour has purchased a cheaper shoe even though it cost him more.

There are a few twists to the above. What if in the two years, you will wear this only for 60 days and your neighbour will wear it for 600 days? The usage also counts.

Another twist. Because the design of the cheaper shoe is bad, there are chances that you will slip and fall and sprain your leg. Doctor's fees may go up to ₹10,000

In short, a cost is just not about the price you pay. There are many factors that you should take into consideration and this type of evaluation is called life-cycle costing.

Some hypothetical examples of life-cycle costing are given at the end of the chapter. What is important is that we consider usage, convenience, affordability, maintenance and other associated costs. It also means, not to get fooled by brands and to ensure that you get value for money.

Does a higher price mean better quality? No, not always. The success of the cost saver is getting something much cheaper to perform the same function. This is one of the objectives the quality movement is supposed to achieve. Improved performance and price reduction simultaneously.

I will share an example with you. I was posted in a malaria prone area. It was very scenic and beautiful but the chance of getting malaria was high. The accommodation that we were given was well ventilated and spacious but there was no netting on the windows. When I went to the local contractor, he was ready to manufacture windows with netting, but the cost was prohibitively high. My wife then suggested a product called 'Netlon'. You tape and nail Velcro around your window. The edges of the Netlon have the clinger and you simply mount the net on the window. Hey presto, the same function was achieved at one-tenth the cost! The only disadvantage is that it takes a little longer to remove the net. Now in this scenario is opening or removing the net important? No! Far better the net remains there all the time. At one-tenth the cost, the same function of keeping out the mosquitos was achieved. My organisation used this same principle for the other houses and the incidence of malaria came down, leading to a savings in medical expenses.

Cost reduction is an exercise that you have to constantly carry out in your personal and professional life. Examples of cost reduction that can be carried out in your everyday life are as follows:

a) Don't eat out or buy food from outside except on occasions. Try to learn cooking. This will save you lots of money and to cook a reasonably good dish does not take you time.

b) Learn to wash and iron your clothes yourself. May sound boring but it is a good work out and will save you money.

c) On the weekend spend time visiting a park instead of a mall.

d) Join a good library and develop the reading habit.

You will probably ask, why should I do all this? Isn't it a waste of time? In a month you will probably save a sum of ₹2,000.

Translated into an annual sum of ₹24,000. When you convert this into a compounded growth at even 7% per annum at the end of thirty years you are talking about a sum of ₹1.83 lakhs.

This is just one of the many examples that we are talking about.

- Cost Savings at times, for corporates is the only alternative between life and death. Here below are a number of live examples of cost saving.
    - Rent versus Outright purchase

        Examples: Renting a desk, renting a room, renting office space instead of purchasing property. This can also be extended to cars, other assets. Even manufacturing capacity can be hired.

        Outsourcing capability versus developing inhouse capability. For certain categories of employees and functions you can outsource this capability. Examples: accounting, taxation, security, property services like electricity and plumbing, transport etc
    - Instead of travelling have online meetings.
    - Instead of buying software see if you can hire software or use software that is free. Spend only if you must.
- Here we will discuss some examples of cost savings which hopefully will make things clear that cheap is not always good. These are real life examples.
    - Somnath has never taken tuition in his life. For his CA final exam, he is a little weak in taxation. There is a very good tutor near his house, but the tutor is expensive. The tutor charges ₹2000 per month. His father tells him that if he qualifies as a CA in his first attempt and starts earning money, say ₹20,000 per month, in six months he will earn ₹1,20,000. Whereas in the six months leading to the exams he will spend only ₹12,000. Moreover, a good tutor will spark an interest and cement his foundations in tax which may

lead to him becoming a top-class tax professional. Somnath listens to his father's advice and aces his tax paper and passes his CA in his first attempt.

o In a huge project costing several hundred crores, the furnace is the most expensive part of the project. The suppliers of the furnace have a condition that the stand on which the furnace rests is to be built by the project owners or the furnace suppliers can build it. Due to safety reasons, the specifications of the furnace stand have to be complied with, to the last bolt. Any small deviation, and the furnace stand can be rejected by the furnace supplier. If the project owners build the stand the cost will be USD 150,000. If the furnace suppliers build it, it will be USD 300,000. The cost of the furnace is USD 60 million. The following are the outcomes if the furnace suppliers reject the furnace stand:

i. The project will be delayed by six months.

ii. Six months of production loss translates into a cash loss of USD 10 million.

This is not a major issue. Any sensible CEO will ask the furnace supplier to make the furnace stand. Not this CEO, he thought he would save USD 150,000 and landed up losing USD 10 million.

- Cost Saving is very important, but don't forget to see the big picture

An example of Life-Cycle Costing

- How does one calculate life-cycle costing?

In our minds we must be very clear as to what function we wish to carry out. Let us now take an example – we want to start a transport agency. Transport of goods come in many shapes and sizes. You have trucks, big trucks and minivans. We now must decide the tonnage. How much do we want to transport at a time?

The range of vehicles is from 0.85 tons to 32 tons.

Obviously, the cost of a 32-ton truck and trailer will be much more than a 0.85-ton capacity truck. So, it is very important that you are clear about the function and the purpose of the truck. The price ranges from ₹4 lakhs to ₹40 lakhs. Hence there is a close co-relation between price and function. Let us say, you have decided to be in the small segment. i.e., 0.85 tons

Option A: Brand X

Capital Cost: ₹4 lakhs

Life is 10 years

Maintenance over lifetime: ₹3 lakhs

Insurance: ₹30,000/year

Diesel/km: ₹5.5

Annual mileage: 20,000 km per annum

Resale value: ₹0

Now let us annualise the costs above

Capital cost per annum = ₹40,000

Maintenance = ₹30,000

Insurance = ₹30,000

Mileage costs = ₹1,10,000

Total annual cost = ₹2,10,000

So, at a glance, you can see your biggest cost is running the mini truck. Hence, when you do your life-cycle costing, you have to see which truck gives you the best mileage. Your decision should revolve around that.

Option B: Brand Y

Capital Cost: ₹6 lakhs

Life is 10 years

Maintenance over lifetime: ₹2 lakhs

Insurance: ₹40,000/year

Diesel/km: ₹4.0

Annual mileage: 20,000 km per year

Resale value = ₹0

Now let us annualise the costs above

Capital cost per annum = ₹60,000

Maintenance = ₹20,000

Insurance = ₹40,000

Mileage costs = ₹80,000

Total annual cost = ₹2,00,000

So, at a glance, you can see your biggest cost is running the truck. Hence, when you do your life-cycle costing you have to see which truck gives you the best mileage. Your decision should revolve around that.

Even though option B has the higher capital cost, the life-cycle costing is cheaper.

If the mileage is more, the difference will be greater.

Over ten years, you save ₹10,000 x 10 = ₹1,00,000 with option B.

Balance Sheet – What Does It Convey?

A balance sheet of an entity conveys, **at a particular point of time,** what the entity is worth. The entity can be an individual, an organization or a huge corporate. Please also see the words highlighted, **'at a particular point of time'**. The worth may change after a month. There may be big developments after that date, that will totally destroy the worth of the individual. It is very important to understand that the worth is valid as on the date of the balance sheet.

Let us take the balance sheet of Mr Surya Prakash, an individual, to know more about what we are trying to convey.

This is the list of assets that Mr Surya Prakash owns on 31.12.2020

Asset	Value in ₹
One Flat in Bangalore	80,00,000
Fixed Deposit in SBI	5,00,000
Shares in ITC	10,00,000
Furniture	75,000
White Goods in the House	25,000
Car	4,00,000
Clothes of self and wife	10,000
Jewellery	2,00,000
Retirement Benefits accrued	75,00,000
Insurance Policies	20,00,000
Total of assets	**1,97,10,000**

List of liabilities

Liability	Value in ₹
Housing Loan from Bank	10,00,000
Loan from friend	2,00,000
Payments due for Insurance policies	1,00,000
Total of liabilities	**13,00,000**

Net worth = Assets - Liabilities = ₹1,84,10,000

Now to comment well on Surya Prakash's net worth, we would also like to know his age. Let us take three different ages. If Surya Prakash is 33 years old, we will all agree that he has been very successful in amassing this wealth at a young age. If Surya Prakash is 50 years old, then we will know that he is moderately successful and since he has ten years left to go before retirement, he can increase his net worth. If he is 60 years old, we will say that his success is above average but not exceptional.

So, when you calculate the net worth of an entity, you should also be prepared to calculate the future earning capacity of the individual.

We shall take a few other examples of individuals and then come to a conclusion about their net worth.

These are the list of assets that Mr Malakar Babu owns on 31.12.2020

Asset	Value in ₹
One Flat in Bangalore	80,00,000
Fixed Deposit in SBI	5,00,000
Shares in ITC	10,00,000
Furniture	75,000
White Goods in the House	25,000

Car	4,00,000
Clothes of self and wife	10,000
Jewellery	2,00,000
Retirement Benefits accrued	75,00,000
Insurance Policies	20,00,000
Total of assets	**1,97,10,000**

List of liabilities

Liability	Value in ₹
Loan from money lender	2,00,00,000
Housing Loan from Bank	10,00,000
Payments due for Insurance policies	1,00,000
Total of liabilities	**2,11,00,000**

Net worth = Assets – Liabilities = – ₹13,90,000

You will observe that the assets of Mr Malakar Babu and that of Surya Prakash are the same. However, the loan that Mr Malakar Babu has taken from a money lender has vitiated his net worth. Mr Malakar Babu had a tip from his doctor friend that there was one medicine that cured COVID-19 and was available. If Mr Malakar Babu could purchase ₹2 crore worth, then in the market, it could be sold for three times the price and Mr Malalkar Babu would make 4 crores in a short period. Mr Malakar Babu went to a money lender and borrowed this money at an annual interest of 25 percent. The tip provided to be a false lead and both Mr Malakar Babu and his friend are in deep trouble. So, one can see how a 'get rich fast' scheme has destroyed the net worth of Mr Malakar Babu.

Again, now to comment well on Malakar Babu's net worth, we would also like to know his age. Let us take three different ages. If he is 33 years old, we will all agree that he has time to recover from this terrible decision. If he is 50 years old, then we will know that he has ten years left to go before retirement, and if he struggles and works hard, there is a chance that he can repay all this debt. If on the other hand he is 60 years old, we can say that he is in deep trouble and can go under. A simple lesson is that your risk-taking capacity changes with time. We are not talking about exceptional cases, only a trend.

Cash cycle of a salaried individual

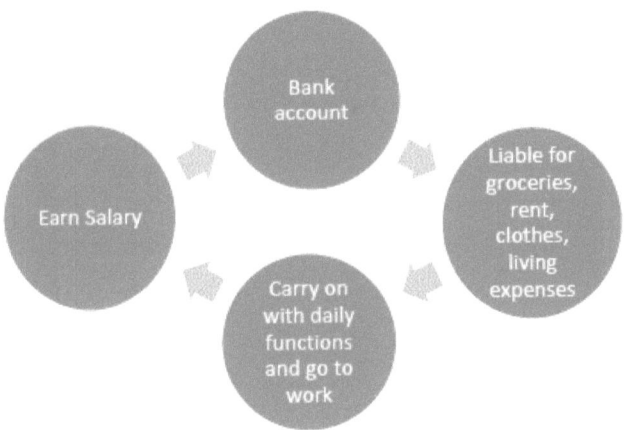

Now we will move from individuals to corporates.

A very important concept here is the working capital cycle. This is something which all of us, irrespective of the size of business, have to understand. If we fail to understand this, it is very difficult to run a business, any business, however big or small it may be. This applies equally well to both manufacture and service.

Explained below is the working capital cycle in a diagrammatic form (read clockwise)

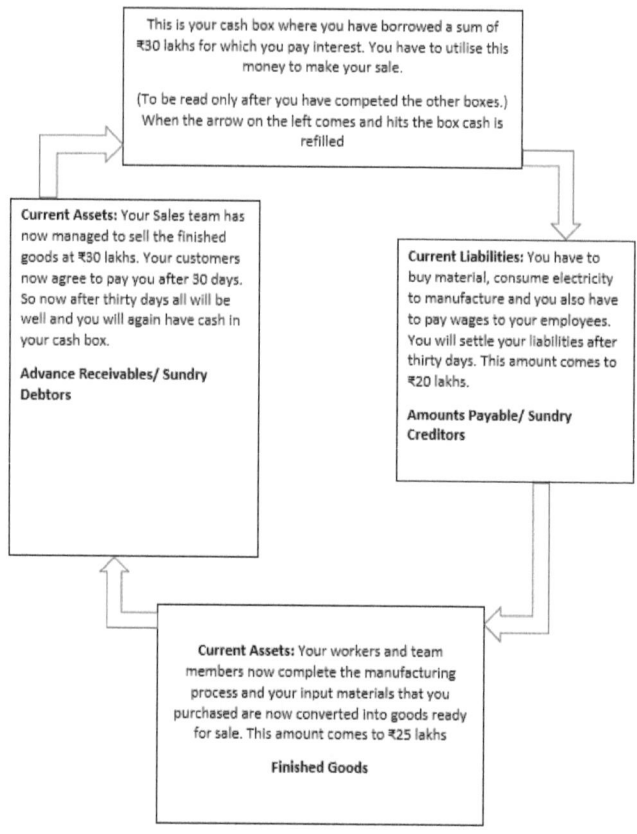

You will see in the illustration that the boxes get bigger and bigger. It has been done deliberately. This is to show value addition at each step. Your employees' efforts for which you pay them the wages, the electricity for which you pay the municipality and the raw material for which you pay your supplier of goods, are combined to make a product or a service worthy of sale. There is also the cost of depreciation of machinery and buildings to be factored in, so your finished goods and services are higher in value than the inputs.

- When you sell, you add a mark-up or profit which makes the next box even bigger.
- The faster you convert this cycle, that is, turn your employees' efforts into cash, the more efficient you are.
- When do the boxes spring a leak? When your employees using the materials are not able to convert the goods into sales. That can happen for many reasons: sub-standard quality, incorrect pricing, or no demand. When your marketing team is unable to sell, the finished goods pile up and are unable to convert into the next level. If your marketing is not able to realise the money from making the sale, the last leg is incomplete, and you do not get cash.
- If the leak is not fixed, you will have to borrow more money; borrowing more money means more interest and less profit. Also, you can only borrow more money up to a point of time. After that, you will run out of money and will have to close your organisation.
- In the next section the effect of a leak will be illustrated.

The Stock Box In The Working Capital Cycle Is Affected

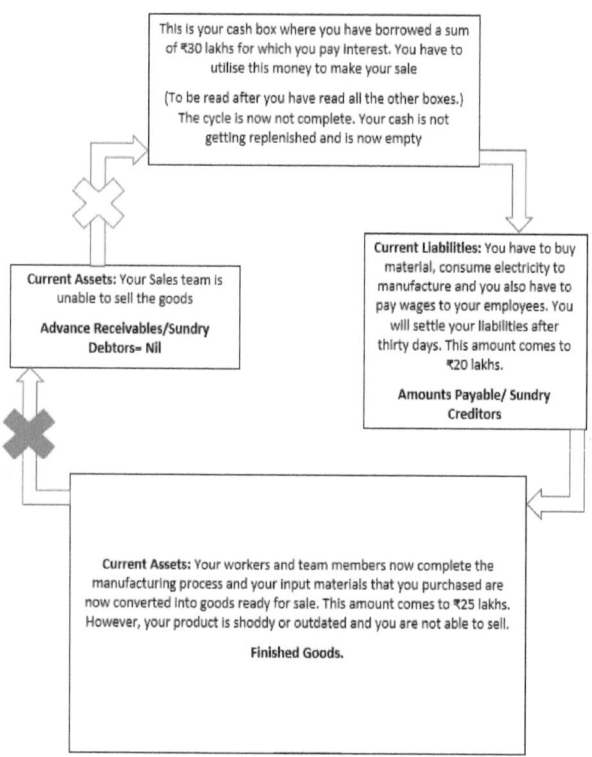

You can see from the illustration above that the stock box has bloated and is sucking all the money into stock. The cycle has now been weakened. The business is unable to generate money efficiently with the result that the money you started with is getting depleted, leaving you with the option to borrow more. You have to examine why your stock is building up. In a service organization substitute Service for Finished Goods.

The Advance Receivable/ Debtors Box In The Working Capital Cycle Is Affected

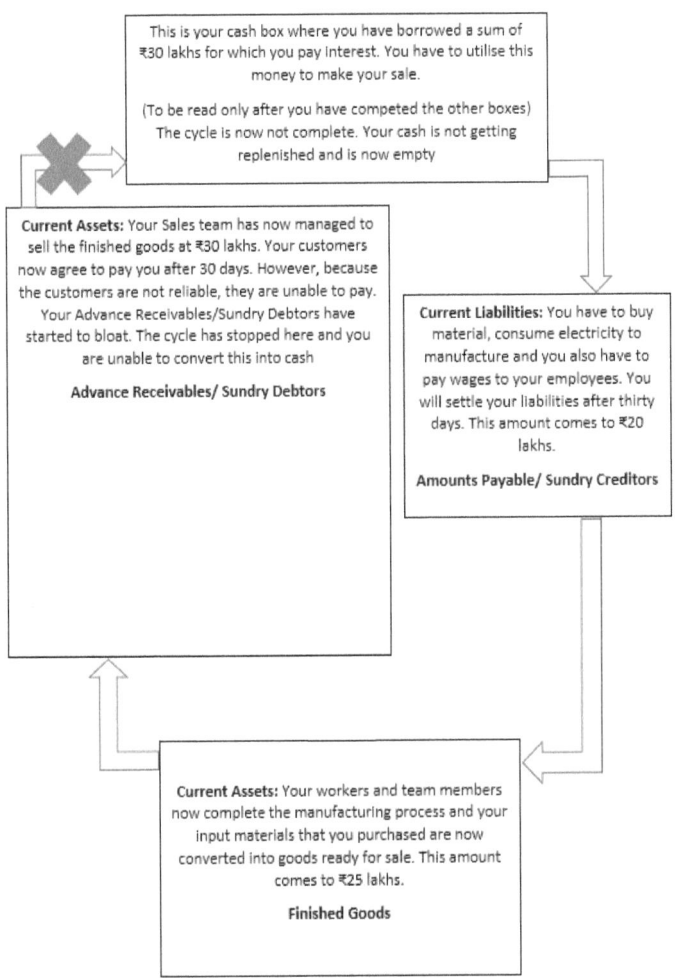

You can see from the illustration above that the debtor's box has bloated and is sucking all the money. The cycle has now been weakened. The business is unable to generate money, leaving you with the option to borrow more.

The Effect Of An Incomplete Cash Cycle

- From the above examples it has become clear what happens when your cash cycle is incomplete. On one hand, you have to continue to pay wages, rent, suppliers of goods and services and on the other hand because of bad management of stock or debtors, the working capital cycle has become inefficient.
- If the problem is not sorted out, you will run out of funds.
- In case you still borrow more, then you will pay costly interest which will eat into your profits.
- Even though the concept is simple, working capital management in most companies is not handled very well.
- Some quick calculations:

    If your annual sales are ₹60 crores and your finished stock is worth ₹20 crores.

    60 crores = 12 months sales

    20 crores = 20/60 x 12 months = 4 months sales

    Simple arithmetic: ₹20 crores, the stock you are carrying is the equivalent of four months sales. Why are you carrying such stock for a period of four months? There is no right or wrong answer. It depends on the business, but anything more than six months stock is a red flag.

    In the same example, if your debtors/receivables are ₹40 crores, they are the equivalent of 40/60 x 12 months = 8 months sales. In debtors, anything over the equivalent of three months sales is considered very inefficient. In the statement of accounts, you have to disclose to your shareholders if the age of the receivables is more than six months. In effect, your customer, instead of borrowing from the bank is financing his business by not paying you on time.

- Do not think that you can reduce your borrowings by not paying your employees and suppliers on time. If your customers don't pay, and there is no money in your top box because it has not been refilled, the solution does not lie in not paying your employees and suppliers. Legislation demands that you pay your workers on time. Not paying your workers will mean shrinkage in employee morale. Some utilities, such as water and electricity, will shut off your supply if you do not pay. As regards your suppliers, remember you not paying them on time will destroy their working capital cycle too. Over a period of time, you will get the reputation of being an irresponsible provider and either your suppliers will not provide goods or services or will increase the prices. Cash management, especially working capital management, is a very important part of your business and more so for start-ups.

- Imagine for a minute, you have purchased a top of the range car. It has got the best features possible. Suddenly you discover that you have not looked at the petrol gauge and you have run out of petrol. This wonderful car with all its beautiful features is now useless. All because you did not look at the petrol gauge. What petrol is to the car, cash is to your business. If you do not monitor your stock levels and debtors (very similar to not looking at the gauge), you will also run out of cash and your business, though of very high potential, will come to a stop.

Balance Sheet Of A Corporate

The Net Worth Of A Corporate

A balance sheet of an entity conveys, **at a particular point of time,** what an entity is worth. As discussed earlier, the worth of any entity is the difference between its assets and the liabilities it owes. It is very important to remember that the worth is valid as on the date of the balance sheet. We had discussed with a few examples what the worth of an individual was. In the case of a corporate, even though the fundamental principle remains the same, there are a few points which we will make clear.

In a corporate, the assets and liabilities are divided into long-term and short-term or current. Normally those which stretch for more than a year are long-term, and those that are for less than a year are short-term. Recapitulating, expenditure whose benefit lasts more than a year is capital expenditure and that which lasts less than a year is revenue expenditure. So, all our assets that last more than a year will be long-term assets. They include machinery, cars, houses etc. What will be our short-term assets? Let us go to our working capital cycle. Stock and debtors will be our current assets. Similarly, what will be a corporate's liabilities? The long-term liabilities will be loans that are to be repaid after more than a year. Current liabilities are those that are in the first box of the working capital cycle, liabilities that you have to settle towards your suppliers, employees and utility providers. The difference between Current Assets and Current Liabilities is called Working Capital.

At this point of time, I would like to introduce one more concept called **'provision'**. A provision is nothing but a liability that has not been quantified.

Let me give you a few examples in an individual's life as well as a corporate's life. Let us say today Shyam's net worth is ₹1 crore. Shyam is a 30-year-old individual married, with one child aged 2 years. Is it correct for Shyam to splurge that ₹1 crore and buy a Mercedes? Debatable point. Some may say, "yes, what is the point in saving for tomorrow, live life today". Someone who is a little more serious and conservative would say Shyam should provide for the child's higher education. If Shyam sets aside ₹50 lakhs to provide for the child's higher education, Shyam's worth falls down to ₹50 lakhs because of the provision.

Corporates have to account for many such provisions. Suppose there is a lawsuit which the corporate is likely to lose. The judgement has not been made as yet, but in all probability the lawyers feel that the company will lose ₹50 crores. Hence, a provision has to be made and depending on how fast the court will decide, it can be short-term or long-term.

To simplify this, a provision is nothing but a liability whose exact value has not been ascertained.

The Balance Sheet of XYZ Private Ltd. is given on the next page.

XYZ PRIVATE LTD.

Assets	Value in ₹
Long term Assets	
Land and Buildings	25,00,000
Plant and Machinery	45,00,000
Current Assets	
Stock	15,00,000
Debtors	10,00,000
Total of assets	**95,00,000**
Liability	Value in ₹
Long term Liabilities	
Long term loans	30,00,000
Current Liabilities	
Suppliers	10,00,000
Utilities	5,00,000
Employees	2,00,000
Total of liabilities	**47,00,000**

Net worth = Assets - Liabilities = ₹48,00,000

Thankfully, you do not have to do this laborious calculation to find the net worth of an audited entity. The difference between the assets and the liabilities is given under the head, **Shareholders' Funds or Owner's Funds** in the balance sheet.

What exactly are shareholders' funds?

A company is an artificial body. If the shares of the company can be freely traded in a stock exchange, it is a limited company and if the shares cannot be freely traded, it is a private limited company. So now we have four distinct entities in a company:

1. The shareholders who own the company.
2. The company itself.
3. The directors of the company, to whom the shareholders have given the responsibility of managing the company.
4. The employees of the company.

Imagine that you start a business and it is totally owned by you. All the profits the business makes belong to you. The capital you invested to start the business belongs to you. Both the capital and the profits belong to you. Similarly, in a company the share capital and the profits of the company belong to the shareholders and not to the company. The company is a separate entity from its shareholders and so you will see in a company's balance sheet the share capital and the profits will be on the liability side, as will be the debts and creditors that the company owes. This is because the company owes this money (share capital and profits) to the shareholders and has no right over it.

Now once again, let us take the example of you starting a business. As the business starts to generate more and more profits, from a totally common-sense perspective, the business becomes more valuable. It is no longer the same business that it was on day one. After a couple of years, people are aware of the business, the business has regular customers and there are loyal customers who patronise the business. All this is reflected in more money being generated by the business. Similarly in a company, the share capital and the profits that the company has generated and retained is called the shareholders' funds or net worth of the company.

Hold on! We have used a word 'retained'. What is that? Let us go back to our old example of the business that you started. You have two options to utilise the profits:

1. Use the profits for personal enjoyment, such as to buy a BMW or go on a holiday to Europe.

2. Keep the profits in the business itself and use it to expand the business.

When you exercise option 1 and use the profits to buy a BMW or go on a holiday and transfer the money to yourself, the business no longer has any right over that money and the money belongs to you. Similarly in a company when the profits are given to the shareholders as dividend, the company no longer has any right over that money. In option 2, when the profits are left with the business or the company, this money is called retained earnings and the money is in the control of the business or the company.

The net worth of a business or company is the sum of capital plus retained earnings and is equal to the difference between the assets and liabilities. If the company is making losses, what then? If the loss is greater than the share capital the net worth will be negative and this shows the liabilities are more than the assets. We will continue our discussion on the assumption that the net worth is positive.

When you divide shareholders' funds by the number of shares you get the book value of the share. Normally the market value is more than the book value of a share.

When the book value is more than the market value, examine the credentials of the promoters and the type of business. If they are good and the business has potential, think of buying that share.

I have done this exercise for one listed company that I have picked at random.

Price to Book Value

Proctor and Gamble Health Ltd

The date is 31.12.2019

The Shareholders' funds are ₹816.81 crores

The number of shares is 1.66 crores

The book value per share is ₹816.81/1.66 = ₹492 per share

The net worth of Proctor and Gamble Health Ltd is ₹492 per share

The market value of the share, that is the price at which the share is trading, is at ten times its book value, that is close to ₹5,000 per share.

This difference between the book value and the market value can be the subject of a doctorate and is not going to be covered in this book. The market perceives that this share has got a great future and part of the price the market is willing to pay is because of the future growth of Proctor and Gamble.

Let us take another example.

The share price of Apple Inc. on 21.05.2021 was $125, the book value $4.

The ratio of the market price of the share to the book value here is 30, in Proctor and Gamble it is 10. What does this ratio convey? It conveys that the shareholders think Apple will grow faster than Proctor and Gamble.

Price-Earnings Ratio

Just like the above ratio which compares the market value of a share to the book value of a share, there is a ratio which compares the market value of a share with the earnings per share. Let us say a company earned a profit of ₹10 million in a particular financial year. The number of shares is 2 million. Each share has earned ₹5 (₹10 million/ 2 million). If the market price of the share is ₹50, the price-earnings ratio is 10 (₹50/₹5, market price/share divided by earning/share).

Let us see what the Price-Earnings ratio of Apple and Proctor and Gamble is.

The Price-Earnings ratio of Apple was 29 on 30.11.2021. The Price to Book value was about 43.

The Price-Earnings ratio of Proctor and Gamble was 26 while the Price to Book value was around 7.

It shows that though at present both companies are earning well, the market expects Apple to do much better than Proctor and Gamble in the future. However, it is very difficult to forecast what will happen. So, don't delve too much into all this.

Here let us pause and try to understand what a balance sheet is trying to convey.

1. As already discussed, a balance sheet tries to convey on a particular date, what an entity (individual or a commercial organization) owns and owes.

2. If the entity owns more than what it owes, subject to some reasonable checks, the entity has grown since inception. On the other hand, if the entity owns less than what it owes, the entity is in debt and in trouble.

   Let us first take the case of an individual, Prasad, who has assets worth ₹60 lakhs and has liabilities worth ₹55 lakhs. His net worth is ₹5 lakhs. If he has liabilities worth ₹70 lakhs, his liabilities exceed his assets. This means that he is close to being bankrupt if he does not take corrective action.

3. There is an important ratio one should be aware of, that is the Debt/Equity ratio. This ratio indicates what the long-term debt divided by the owner/shareholder's fund or net worth is. In the example of XYZ private Ltd. above, the long-term debt is ₹30 lakhs and the net worth is ₹48 lakhs. It is good, as Debt/Equity ratio is less than one. Normally this ratio is industry specific, but as a thumb rule, anything less than one is good and anything more than one is risky.

If in the case of a salaried individual, his debt is more than what he owns, the question we must ask is, what is the debt for? If it is a house, an asset is being built, and as he pays off his liability, his liability will come down and his assets will go up. On the other hand, if the debt is for a car, the value of the car will depreciate and over time both liability and asset will come down, leading him to what he was earlier. There will be no growth in his assets. The risk of taking debt has been explained elsewhere.

4. Very briefly, both in our personal and professional life, we must analyse clearly why we are taking debt. At times taking debt is good, but, as a general rule, we must take debt as a last resort and only if we are building up assets.

Prior to concluding this topic, a few clarifications:

- Sundry Debtors and Accounts Receivables are the same. Either term may be used in a particular country, but they essentially mean the same thing – the money your customers owe you when they have purchased goods on credit.

- Similarly, Sundry Creditors and Accounts Payable mean the same thing. The mirror image of Sundry Debtors and Accounts Receivable i.e., the amount payable by you or your organisation for buying other people's/organization's goods on credit. A Sundry Debtor/ Accounts Receivable in your books will be a Sundry Creditor/ Account Payable in your customer's books.

I do hope that with this the balance sheet is no longer a black box but a simple statement about the worth of a company on any particular date.

Cash Flows

In our opinion, the single most important commercial skill in running a business is to understand cash flows. If you have grasped working capital management, you have grasped 80 to 90% of understanding cash flows. We shall try to illustrate this in the form of an example and then go to what this important topic is all about.

Let us say you are looking for a prospective business partner. However, you would like to know the credentials of the person you are planning to do business with. One person rings you up and tells you that he will pick you up from your house and will conduct the meeting in a posh restaurant. At the appointed time, the person appears at your doorstep in a chauffeur driven Mercedes and discusses the plan with you over a dinner in a five-star hotel. He is very suave and well-dressed. You are taken up by him and agree to team up with him. You speak to your close friend who is a bit cynical, and he tells you that the best way to judge his wealth is to see his bank balance. You get a shock when you see his bank balance, which has been shown to you surreptitiously by your neighbourhood banking friend. You find out that this person does not have much money to his name and had hired a Mercedes and chauffeur for a few hours to impress you.

The point is that all numbers can be tweaked or misrepresented, except cash or your bank balance. Bank balance can very easily be verified. A cash flow statement tells you exactly from where you have got your money and how you have spent it. This tells you how well or badly your business is doing. Cash flows are easy to understand.

Illustrated below are cash flow statements of two college students.

Kalyan lives the high life though he is the son of a middle-class government officer. Many of his college mates think he is the son of a rich man.

Cash flow of Kalyan, a second year B.Com. student in Loyola College, for the month of November 2020 is given below. Sources of funds tells you where the money came from, and Utilization of funds tells you where the money has been spent.

Source of funds	Value in ₹
Pocket money from father	1000
Loan from Guru	500
Loan from Saurav	500
Total of inflows	**2000**
Utilization	Value in ₹
Cigarettes	200
Pub	600
Dinner with girlfriend	600
Part repayment of loan to Raju	300
Part repayment of loan to Ram	300
Total of outflows	**2000**

Let us try to see what this statement conveys

- The first red flag is that against a pocket money of ₹1000, Kalyan is spending ₹2000. He is leading a high life, visiting pubs, smoking, and dining with his girlfriend.
- This, is in the long run will cause him grief.
- Part of his loan money of ₹1000 has gone to repay loans to other people whom he has borrowed money from. This shows that Kalyan is a very persuasive individual. From this statement, we can draw a conclusion that four

students have lent him money. There may be others who have given him money before but have not been repaid as yet, but we do not know this because the cash flow is for one month.

- Against a sum of ₹1000 of pocket money, he is spending ₹1400, burning a hole in his pocket of ₹400. If he does this regularly, his debts would be ₹4800 in a year. His father can barely afford to send him ₹1000. He will get his father into deep trouble because his father would have to cough up this money.

So, one can see what a simple cash flow statement can reveal about an individual. Obviously, his father is paying his college fees and mess bills directly. If someone makes a statement like this for Kalyan and explains things to him, including the fact that his father is making great sacrifices to send him to college, it may change his habits.

Let us now see a similar statement for Manoj, who also is a second year B.Com. student.

Source of funds	Value in ₹
Pocket money from father	200
From tuitions	500
From part-time job	500
Total of inflows	**1200**
Utilization	Value in ₹
Mess bill in hostel	600
Money sent back to father	600
Total of outflows	**1200**

Obviously, this guy is a serious individual and must be coming from a lower middle-class family. He is keeping his expenditure under check while contributing to the family.

As in the case of an individual, cash flows of corporates tell us a lot about the corporate, which a balance sheet may not be able to reveal.

We must note a few simple points before we analyse the cash flow of corporates or business houses.

When your stock or debtors increase, is it a cash inflow or outflow?

- An increase of debtors and stock represents an outflow of cash. A decrease of debtors or stock represents a cash inflow. For a shopkeeper, increase in number of shirts (stock) only happens if he has spent money to buy them. Similarly, decrease in shirts means that he has sold them and he has got money.
- A profit means money has come in and it represents an inflow.
- Increase of borrowings means inflows. You borrow money, cash comes in. You repay your loans, cash goes out. A decrease in borrowings means cash outflows.

From the above we come across these generic rules:

1. Increase in assets, current and long-term, means cash outflows
2. Decrease in assets, current and long-term, means cash inflows
3. Increase in liabilities, current and long-term, means cash inflows
4. Decrease in liabilities, current and long-term, means cash outflows
5. Profit means cash inflow
6. Loss means cash outflow

We are now ready to examine the cash flow of a start-up in its first year of operations.

Start-up ABC Ltd has the following cash flow statement for the year ending March 2019, which happens to be the first year.

Inflows	In ₹ crore
Venture capital	2.00
Promoter's equity	0.50
Profit from operations	0.25
Increase in creditors for goods	0.50
Total of inflows	**3.25**
Outflows	In ₹ crore
Plant and machinery	0.50
Increase in debtors	0.75
Increase in finished stock	1.00
Laptops	0.25
Increase in purchased stock	0.75
Total of outflows	**3.25**

This is a simple cash flow that you need to prepare. In any business, new or old, cash is king and you must conserve cash. The COVID-19 epidemic knocked out many businesses mainly because they had not kept a healthy cash reserve. Let us now examine what the cash flow statement says.

The working capital management seems to be out of control. It has taken away ₹2 crores of cash.

Sum of increase in debtors, finished stock, purchased stock (₹2.50 crore), less increase in creditors (₹0.50 crore) gives us the Net Working Capital = ₹2.00 crore.

As we have discussed earlier, increase in assets means that you have a cash outflow. How do we know that this increase in debtors and finished stock is justified or not?

Let us say the sales for that year were ₹2 crore.

Recollecting the formula we had discussed, let us convert the debtors to months of sales:

0.75 crores ÷ 2 crores x 12 months = 4.5 months of sales

The first red flag has popped up. We had mentioned that the normal thumb rule is that your debtors should not exceed three months. Now let us analyse this further. How old are the debtors? You call your accountant and your sales manager to discuss this. The sales manager tells you that ₹0.50 cores of debtors is because of a sale that took place during the previous month, and ₹0.25 crores is over six months old. There has been no follow-up from the sales team because they were all busy with trying to meet the sales target. Now one can safely say that the ₹0.25 crores is in jeopardy. You must tell your sales team that making a sale is not enough but that one must also collect the cash to complete the sales cycle.

Now, let us examine the finished stock. The finished stock has gone up by a crore. Using the same logic as above 1 crore ÷ 2 crore x 12 months = 6 months. This means that your finished stock is the equivalent of 6 months. Why have we blocked up our money in producing six months stock? Your sales team says that in the next six months because of COVID-19, the sales team cannot sell more than two months stock. Sales have plunged. You then have to take a call whether to stop production to liquidate the stock. The labour will be idle. You can perhaps negotiate for half pay. It may have been best for you to have hired capacity in a unit that is already manufacturing. Now, another familiar concept should strike you with which you should corelate. If you have started your own production unit, your labour will be fixed cost, but when you hire capacity in another unit, it becomes variable.

One more point we must consider is that in our sources of funds, by not paying our creditors we are funding our outflows. We may lose our goodwill and suppliers may not give us credit any more. These are important issues that we should examine and check for how long we have not paid our creditors.

Cooking the books

I am sure many of you would have heard of the Enron scandal. Closer home, the Satyam scandal made headlines. What happened in both these cases? The books of accounts, and so the financial statements, showed a far rosier picture than what was actually happening. The auditors were careless. In the case of Arthur Anderson, Enron's auditors, they were held responsible for the debacle and because of the large claim against them, they went bankrupt. In the case of PricewaterhouseCoopers, Satyam's auditors, they managed to evade any claim for damages.

Cooking the books is not easy. It is an example of the adage, that one has to tell a hundred lies to cover one lie. When one cooks the books, lots of loose ends pop up, which can easily be identified by someone who examines the accounts carefully.

Prior to elaborating more on cooking the books, there is an old saying used by accountants, 'sales is vanity, profit is sanity and cash is reality'. What does this mean? You can have higher sales by selling goods much below market price. This means you will not be able to make high profits unless you are in a near monopoly situation. If your low price does not even cover your costs, this will mean that you will be losing money. So, does high sales at the cost of lower profits or no profit make sense? Is it sustainable? Unfortunately, this simple bit of common-sense is often ignored. For some reason, everyone is interested in higher sales and co-relates increase in sales with growth. Hence the term, 'sales is vanity'. Now sales only make sense if they can be translated to profit for the organization. The ultimate aim for the business is to make profit. If sale does not translate to profit for the organization, the sale is of not much use. Hence the term, 'profit is sanity'. At the end of the day, you need cash to run your business. The working capital cycle has been explained to you. Your business has to convert goods to cash. If your business is unable to convert activities into cash, your business will collapse. Cash is something you see very clearly in your bank account or stashed in a suitcase under your bed. So, 'cash is reality'. If your business has cash which is obvious to everyone, your business is successful. If not, you are very close to bankruptcy.

Coming back to cooking the books, you can paint a rosy picture and fool your investors, creditors, etc., but sooner or later you will be caught if you do not have cash. You can generate cash by borrowing, but this will also become visible in the end, as you will have to pay the interest as well as repay the principal. Fugitives like Mallya and Choksi come to mind. They ran their businesses lavishly by borrowing money and when they could borrow no more money, they tried to run away.

So, when sales are inflated falsely, you have an increase in Sundry Debtors/ Account Receivables, but no cash. When you show huge profits understating expenditure, again the question arises, where is the cash? If you have the cash, have your loans increased? As can be seen, cooking the books is not easy and some loose ends will pop up.

Cash and Accrual Basis

You only record entries in your books of accounts on cash basis. When you give credit to customers or receive credit from suppliers, you record them elsewhere and only when you receive or pay cash, do you account for them in your books. This practice may tell you whether you have enough cash or not and may make the whole organization alert to the fact that they are running out of cash. However, this will not give you a true picture of your profit or loss. When this practice is followed, it is called the cash system.

Let us say you have committed to the fact that you are going to pay your workers a huge bonus in the following April. This is at the year-end subject to the fact that they record a given production in March. You will pay them in April, but your accounting year ends in March. You are paying them for the production they have achieved in March. Is it correct to account this expenditure in the next financial year when you pay cash? In the accrual system, you provide for this expenditure in March. When you account in your books on the commitment that has been made, irrespective of when you pay, your books are written on the accrual system.

Shopkeepers and traders run their small businesses on cash basis. It may suit them, unlike big business, whose accounts are prepared on accrual basis.

Discounted Cash Flows

Does money have a time value?

You have a rich uncle who is a multi-billionaire and is very fond of you. He gives you the following options:

Option 1 - He will give you ₹5 lakhs tomorrow.

Option 2 - He will give you ₹5 lakhs after one year.

Option 3 - He will give you ₹5 lakhs after three years.

You do not understand finance and you start thinking on the following lines:

If you exercise Option 1, you are worried that you will spend the entire money at once. You do not wish to receive 5 lakhs now. What about Option 2 or Option 3? Option 3 is five years away. Anything can happen after five years. You and your uncle may not be on the same terms as now. Option 2 is a safer option. You will get this money in a year. You would, by that time, have thought on how to utilise the money. You will not fritter it away. You discuss this with your financially savvy friend, and he advises you to take the money right away and invest it at once in the post office at approximately 7% interest. He tells you, after doing a small calculation, that after one year, before tax you will get ₹5,35,000 and after five years, you will get ₹7,00,000 assuming the rate of interest remains 7%. You are surprised that such a risk-free investment is giving you so much money. So, what we want to convey through this example, is that money never remains static unless you have stuffed it in your mattress or your pillow cover. There too, money will not be static, because it can be stolen or can be eaten by termites. Value of money increases (if invested wisely) or decreases with time. Since money has a time value, you should base your calculations on this time value. Such a calculation is called discounted cash flow.

Why discounted cash flow? Over time, the money you receive today, if not invested well, loses value. As we saw in the example above, money received today, after one year and after five years is not the same. The same ₹5,00,000 after one year becomes ₹5,35,000 and after five years becomes ₹7,00,000. So, if you do not invest your money wisely and stash it under your pillow, you have to compare ₹5,00,000 with ₹5,35,000 and ₹5,00,000 with ₹7,00,000. To keep things simple, I have not considered inflation.

Now, let us assume, that your uncle gives you the ₹5 lakhs tomorrow and you decide to start your own business. You sit with your finance friend and do some calculations. The worth of your business after one year is ₹5,10,000 and after five years is ₹6,00,000. Does it make sense to invest in a risky business venture? Shouldn't you put it in the post office as a deposit instead? Makes sense, doesn't it? You want adventure and life is too dull. Well, then join an adventure sport and invest your money in the post office. To do business, you have to be ready to take an informed financial risk.

To understand discounted cash flow, one has to appreciate the wonders of compound interest. This is a message to all the young individuals who read this book. Compound interest works exponentially. DO NOT get taken in by stories of those who make a quick buck. For every one individual who makes a quick buck, there are many hundreds who lose a buck even faster. Anyway, without further ado let us see this wonder of compound interest.

You start with ₹10 lakhs and decide to invest this in a bank deposit where the interest rate is 7%.

At the end of the first year, ignoring taxes, the money you have invested will be ₹10.70 lakhs.

Let us put this in a mathematical formula, to see what happens over the years.

Initial sum is ₹10 lakhs

Rate of interest = 7% = 7/100 = 0.07

Interest for one year at 7 percent is 0.07 x 10 lakhs = 0.70 lakhs

So, the principal plus interest will be ₹10.70 lakhs

This can be put as: $10(1+0.70)^1$

At the end of the second year, going by the same logic, the sum will be 10.70(1+0.70) and if we put 10.70 as 10(1+0.70) so at the end of the second year it will be 10(1+0.70)(1+0.70) which is nothing but $10(1.70)^2$

We start off at year 0 (present time)

At year 0 → $10(1+0.07)^0$ = 10 lakhs

At year 1 → $10(1+0.07)^1$ = 10.70 lakhs

At year 2 → $10(1+0.07)^2$ = 11.45 lakhs

At year 3 → $10(1+0.07)^3$ = 12.25 lakhs

At year 7 → $10(1+.0.07)^7$ = 16.06 lakhs

At year 10 → $10(1+0.07)^{10}$ = 19.67 lakhs

Just by keeping it in the bank, your money has doubled.

At year 20 → $10(1+0.07)^{20}$ = 38.69 lakhs

In another 10 years your money will increase to almost 4 times.

At year 30 → $10(1+0.07)^{30}$ = 76.12 lakhs

In another 10 years, your money has increased about 7 times.

At year 40 → $10(1+0.07)^{40}$ = 149.74 lakhs

In another 10 years, your money has increased to 15 times!

Let us say instead of ₹10 lakhs you had invested ₹1 crore. At the end of 40 years, your money would have become ₹15 crores.

Nobody can see the future, but there have been people who have made much more money by investing in businesses or in the stock exchange or in property or in gold. There have been many more people who have lost whatever they had by investing in the above entities. One must do one's homework well and invest wisely. What does all this have to do with discounted cash flows?

We have seen above that, ₹10 lakhs invested, becomes ₹149.74 lakhs in 40 years.

Let us put it in a form like this:

$149.74 = 10 (1+0.07)^{40}$

Let us make this universal,

$T_n = T_o(1+r)^n$

T_n being the sum after n years

T_o being the sum initially invested

r being the rate of interest that your money should fetch you

To make our multiplication and calculations easy, let us come up with a formula.

If after 1 year we want ₹1 and at 7% rate of interest, what should be the money that we should invest today?

$T_n = 1$

$r = 0.07$

$n = 1$

$\Rightarrow 1 = T_o(1.07)^1$

$T_o = 1 \div 1.07 = 0.93$

So, if we invest ₹0.93 today, at the rate of 7%, we will get ₹1 at the end of one year.

Assuming that there is a safe risk-free opportunity, the money of ₹1 at the end of one year is the equivalent of ₹0.93 today. You may have heard the term present value tables and the present value of money. This is it.

So, when you receive ₹50,000 after one year, the present value of that money is: 50,000 x 0.93 = ₹46,500

When you multiply the amount by 0.93 you reduce or discount the cash flow and hence the term, **discounted cash flows**.

We can prepare the present value tables for five years at 7% rate of interest.

$T_n = T_o(1+r)^n$

So, ₹1 after one year will mean you will invest ₹0.93 today

$1 = T_o(1+0.07)^1$

$T_o = 1/1.07 = 0.93$

₹1 after two years will mean you will invest ₹0.87 today

$1 = T_o(1+0.07)^2$

$T_o = 1/1.145 = 0.87$

₹1 after three years will mean you will invest ₹0.82 today

₹1 after four years will mean you will invest ₹0.76 today

₹1 after five years will mean you will invest ₹0.71 today

You do not have to prepare these discounted cash flow factors as they have already been prepared and you can access the tables easily.

Let us rework an example we had taken earlier without discounting cash flows. In this example we are using 7% because here we have a choice of investing this money at this rate which is risk-free.

You have a choice between buying a washing machine or paying for a maid. For simplicity, let us assume the following – the washing machine and the maid use the same amount of detergent and that electricity costs of the house are reimbursed to you by your company. So, it only boils down to the capital cost of the washing machine and the salary you pay your maid servant. If you do not consider the opportunity cost of investing your money of ₹20,000 in a fixed deposit at 7%, you are indifferent to buying a washing machine or paying ₹4,000 annually to your maid servant for 5 years. The moment you consider the opportunity cost, it makes sense to invest your money in the bank deposit and pay your maid servant.

Today you buy a washing machine and shell out ₹20,000 and you pay your maid the equivalent of ₹4,000 annually for five years.

Year	Pay out if washing machine is bought ₹	Pay out if maid is hired ₹	Present value factor	Present value of outflows ₹
0	20000	4000	1.00	4000
1		4000	0.93	3720
2		4000	0.87	3480
3		4000	0.82	3280
4		4000	0.76	3040
Total	20000	20000		17520

If you see the above table and consider the present value of paying your maid versus buying a washing machine it makes economic sense to invest your money and not buy a washing machine.

In case you have borrowed money to pay for this washing machine, the opportunity cost will not be the rate at which you have invested but the rate at which you have borrowed. Since the borrowing cost is always more than the interest received on a fixed deposit, it becomes more economical to hire a maid.

Amortization Of Costs

In today's world everything is dynamic. Nothing stays still over time. Technology or the environment may change from when you start your business to a year later. Your balance sheet will change on a day-to-day basis. There will be money that you have paid for some asset, for which you expect to get a benefit over five years, and so account for it over five years, then you are amortizing the cost over five years. Let us say, you buy a license fee for a software that is valid for a period of five years. The payment is ₹1,00,000. From our first lesson, the expenditure is capital i.e., it will go to the balance sheet. This benefit will last over five years, so we will expense ₹20,000 to the profit and loss account each year. This is an example of amortization of costs. Now let us say after one year, the software has become outdated. You will then expense the entire ₹80,000 remaining to the profit and loss account. Hence, the lesson is, when you start your business, in the early days, try your best to not create assets that last over a year. Could you have hired the software for a year or used open-source software? We go back to the familiar story, which is, try to see that your costs are variable and not fixed at the beginning of your business.

When you amortize the cost of plant and machinery over its useful life, it is called depreciation. For other assets, it is called amortization.

Accounting Standards

If you examine the companies listed on the stock exchange, they represent diverse businesses. Their shares trade on a common platform. The stock exchange prices a share on many parameters, such as **profits, long-term growth, return on investments, stability of the organization, etc.**

There are many more parameters, but most of them can be seen from the statements of accounts. The preparation of the statements of accounts has to be on uniform principles. If each organization decides to prepare the statements on different sets of assumptions, comparison becomes difficult. So that there is uniformity in preparing them, we have accounting standards. In different countries the accounting standards are different. There is an attempt being made by the accounting bodies to make a uniform accounting standard across the world. That will take time, but the Indian accounting body (Institute of Chartered Accountants of India) ensures that the audited accounts prepared in India have uniform accounting standards or rules.

Selling On Credit – Pitfalls

Out of all the topics that we have included here, this is the second most important, the most important being the working capital cycle. If this topic along with the working capital cycle is clear, then you have got your money's worth, and the book has achieved its purpose. The concept is simple, but very few people understand the pitfalls of selling on credit.

Think back to your college days. Many of us may have experienced one of these:

- Lent money to someone and not got it back
- Borrowed money from someone and not repaid it

Well, if this has not happened to you at all, you have lived a good and blameless life. Most of us do not live such good lives and have either gained or lost because of debts. It is likely that you would have lent and lost. In the working capital cycle, if you recollect the receivables box, where your customers do not pay, your working capital cycle suffers.

In the example above, in college, the money you would have lost would have been small. Let us say you start your business. Your first sale is ₹5 lakhs and your customer does not pay. What do you do? File a lawsuit? The lawsuit in all probability will cost you more than ₹5 lakhs, not to mention the time spent in doing the rounds of the court. If your profit is ₹50,000 on the above transaction, then the profit of ten such transactions are wiped out. It is very important that you get your money back every time that you sell. How do you ensure this?

Your bank can play a big role in this, and we will discuss the major safety nets that we can put in place to ensure that your customer pays you the money.

1. Letter of Credit: This is the most popular instrument. This is used for a big value sale. If you are selling ₹10 lakhs worth of rice to a customer in New York, there can be two unwanted scenarios:

    i. After the sale takes place, your customer does not pay.
    ii. After the customer gives you the money, you do not supply the goods, or you supply sub-standard goods.

    In both cases, it is not a win-win situation. The bank steps in and tells you that if you ship standard goods of quality acceptable to the buyer and give the bank the proof, the bank will pay you the money on behalf of the customer. The bank takes this responsibility and does this act through a letter of credit. The bank also tells the customer to give the bank the money and the bank will ensure that quality goods have been shipped and only after this is ensured, the bank will pay the money to the supplier. The bank will also ask the customer as to who should inspect the goods that are ready for shipment. There are independent third-party inspection agencies who will certify the quantity and quality of goods shipped for a nominal fee. The same letter of credit ensures that this is done. Normally, the buyer opens a letter of credit of the approximate value of the goods with their bank and this letter of credit is sent to the seller's bank.

2. Cash against Documents: In this case, the goods are indirectly under the control of the bank and the bank will not give the goods to the customer until money is received. The pitfall is that if the customer decides not to collect the goods, in that case the bank is stuck with the goods and will charge you money for storage. The trick is to take about 20% advance from the customer for the goods. Now even if the customer refuses to pay the balance 80%, you can easily sell the goods at 80% of the value as it will be a bargain for another customer. Also,

logically, no customer would like to lose the 20% advance paid.

The background of margin money is being discussed very briefly, with specific reference to cash against documents. In a housing loan, the loan provider normally insists that the buyer of the house pays 20% of the value of the house and the loan provider makes available the balance 80% of the value of the house. However, 100% of the value of the house is hypothecated to the loan provider. This ensures that if the receiver of the loan defaults, the loan provider is not in an adverse position. The loan provider can easily recover the money lent and all administrative costs associated with it. It also demonstrates the commitment the borrower has towards repayment of the loan. This 20% of the payment is referred to as margin money. The same principle is being applied when you make a sale using the cash against documents procedure. The above figure of 20% is just for illustration, the percentage can vary.

3. In case you have no option but to sell without security as discussed, do a due diligence or assessment of the customer's credit worthiness. Check up with existing vendors if this person honours his creditors. Does he pay on time? Try to find out as much as you can about the customer. Make it clear that the second sale will take place on credit only if the money due on the first is completely received.

Have a policy with your marketing team as to how much your exposure to credit for each customer will be. If you are dealing with the government or with a company of repute, it is unlikely that they will not pay. You can take your invoice to the bank and the bank will give you money against this, for which they will charge interest. This is called bill discounting,

The idea is not to convey that selling on credit is bad or dangerous, but one should know the inherent risks associated with selling on credit and how best to mitigate this risk. Train yourself and your team to distinguish between safe and risky/unknown customers. Do not allow your judgement to be clouded by a big value sale. A sale is complete ONLY when the money is received.

Financing The Business: Equity And Debt

How do you finance your start-up? Well, frankly this is a tough question. All that can be said is over the years, many first-generation entrepreneurs have been successful, and lack of finance has not stood in their way of becoming a success. Today, as compared to even a decade back, financing has become much easier. Earlier, unsuccessful companies drowned in a sea of debt and their promoters had to fight with their backs to the wall. Today, if you have had equity financiers, you can walk away from the disaster only a little bruised. There have been promoters who have been unscrupulous in the past as well. There was a case of share capital being raised in Victorian London to convert cobwebs to gold. The shares were oversubscribed. Fame and riches don't sit on the shoulders of every entrepreneur. They are very choosy and will only sit on the shoulders of a chosen few.

Earlier, most borrowings for businesses were through banks. Today, financing has largely moved out of banks to Venture Capitalists (VC) and Private Equity (PE) players. They will lend at high risk to themselves but demand a part of the equity. Financing of a start-up at various stages has been briefly discussed below.

Ramodhar Prasad, a bright young guy who has just finished his education from a premier institute, decides that he no longer wants to join a corporate or a bank, but wants to start something on his own. He has an idea which he feels will be a commercial success. The idea is to make a breakfast mix that has all the vitamins, proteins, fibre with good taste. It can be made ready by adding a cup of boiling hot water to the bowl with the breakfast powder. His uncle, who is a doctor, has told him after analysing it, that it can be certified as having all the necessary nourishment for an adult human being. Ramodhar Prasad had seen his mother make this for his father on days when he was in a tearing hurry and wanted to leave the house well-fed. His father also went on long trips to UK and Europe and was very fussy about his diet. His mother would pack this mix in different packets for each day of travel and all his father had to do was add hot water. Ramodhar had also tasted this and found it tasty. His mother would change the flavour by changing the spices. In today's fast paced world, especially for working youngsters and students, this mix would be a big boon. All someone had to do was get up and after getting ready for office, add hot water to the container in which the product was packed. The bowl in which the product would be packed would be environment friendly and not react at all with the food. The person buying this product need not even have a kitchen. The packet would be sold in sets of five bowls of different flavours. Perfect for a five-day week.

1. Idea Stage

The above is called the idea stage. Ramodhar has many advisors who tell him that it will not work. They say he would have to compete with established brands like Kellogg's. The market is filled with such products. Ramodhar, however, is confident. He has saved ₹10 lakhs and his elder brother promises him another ₹10 lakhs and Ramodhar takes the dive. At this stage, the entrepreneur is alone, and funds will not be so forthcoming from outsiders, and the business has to be funded mainly by oneself or family and friends. At the idea stage, the business can also be funded by 'crowd funding'. Crowd funding is a concept where money is raised from family, friends as well as other people. The individuals contribute relatively small amounts, but the number of people is large, so the amount raised could be substantial.

Venture capitalists will want to see if there is merit in the idea before they invest. They want to see some sort of commitment from the promoter. Ramodhar, hence, uses the ₹20 lakhs to start his business. He has rented a garage in the outskirts of Bengaluru and has got small machines to make the mixture and to pack the mixture in the bowls and seal them. He has spoken to his contacts and friends who have promised him that they will try his product and if it is good, they will buy and recommend it. Ramodhar realises that in this business, quality is everything and he along with his fiancé, take great care in selecting the raw material and they try to use a scientific process in making it. Even though it is his mother's recipe, he has taken great pains to study the way she makes it and has documented the process well. The product does well and Ramodhar has a monthly turnover of ₹5 lakhs. He sells this product under the brand name of 'Tandarust'. He is now confident of approaching a venture capitalist. It is very important to understand that now the business is no longer valued at ₹20 lakhs, the sum Ramodhar had started this business with. Now that the company has a loyal customer base and has proved itself to be viable, its value will be more than the invested amount.

2. Seed Stage

This is the stage where other individuals or external funds are ready to fund the business. Out of convention, the funding from venture capitalists (VCs) is quantified in USD million. There are various terms used to classify investors at this stage.

- Angel Investor: A rich individual or individuals who will buy into your equity. They will be ready to contribute up to USD one million (approximately ₹750 lakhs) depending on the proposal and plan. Other than contribution of money, they will not add much value to your business.

- Incubator: This VC, in addition to money, will also guide on the product design and marketing.

- Accelerator: This VC, in addition to product design and marketing, will help set up functions of accounting, purchase, HR, etc. In other words, they will set up a formal business platform from where you will launch your organization.

- Seed: This VC is a single contributor who will only provide money. The key difference between an angel investor and a seed fund is that an angel investor is an individual, but a seed fund is an institution.

What has changed now? After Ramodhar has received seed money, he no longer operates from the garage. He now operates from a small factory in an industrial area of Bengaluru. The factory has workers, and professionals have been employed. It is no longer a proprietorship but a private limited company. While Ramodhar and his wife retain the controlling stake, the VC also has some people on the board. Ramodhar should know that even though he has got a lot of funds, this is not the time to splurge but keep a tight check on the budget and funds. The VC representative on the board also ensures that all money is spent productively.

The sales turnover of the company has moved from a few lakhs to a few crores. The product is now selling in a few supermarkets. The valuation of the company has increased considerably.

3. **Early stage**

First part of the early stage – Series A: At this stage, the VC is ready to contribute anywhere from USD 3 to 5 million. The product is ready to be launched into the market. Many major decisions have to be taken. Will the product be sold online or will it be a combination of online and direct selling? What will be the price? Will it follow the conventional model of distribution: wholesaler, distributor and retailer? What would be the position of this breakfast food versus others in the market? As the sales increase and the sales now move out of Bengaluru and Mysuru to other cities in Karnataka, there is further requirement of funds. With each funding the valuation of the business is increasing. The sales have increased from a few crores to tens of crores.

Second part of the early stage – Series B: At this stage, the VC will contribute USD 7 to 10 million. Now Ramodhar is ready to go all-India. His earlier breakfast packet was mainly for people from South India. Now he is ready to cater to all tastes. He has introduced lunch and dinner options. He has also introduced healthy snack items. Ramodhar is sticking to his initial principles – little or no preservatives, top quality ingredients and a strong manufacturing process. His strength is that he is delivering a superior product which is healthy and is well packed. With every successive contribution from the VC, the valuation of the company increases.

4. Growth Stage

This attracts the Series C investors. These VCs are ready to contribute USD 20 million. Now these VCs also buy equity, but they pay a much higher price. The company's share of ₹10 is now valued close to ₹100. Ramodhar is no longer a small-scale player. His factory has expanded, and he is now thinking of setting up a second factory in Bhopal. The range of products that are manufactured is wider. Here the organization is able to cover fixed costs and its unit economics is positive. Each successive contribution from here on can be called Series D, E, F, etc. The contribution by investors is higher and also the value of equity keeps increasing as the company is now being valued higher and higher.

5. Late Stage

This is the stage where Private Equity (PE) comes in, the stage before the company becomes public. Here at the late stage, the contribution from the PE players will be USD 50 million. Now Ramodhar has got factory managers from good engineering colleges and marketing guys from premier institutes. His products have a considerable market share, and he is now hailed as one of the successes of food businesses in India. He is well-grounded about his success. He knows that the success that he has got is because of ethical practices, good planning, top class quality control and above all competitive pricing coming from tight and well-planned budgeting. He is not overmanned, and he has realised the importance of efficient delegation and having an excellent reporting system. After a couple of years, he will be ready to go public.

The flip side of funding

We have tracked Ramodhar's progress from a small unit in the garage to a big national player. This success story happens to one entrepreneur in a thousand. If you are going to chase fame and money, you will come to grief. On the other hand, if you love your task and truly want to make a difference to your life and others, there is a good probability that you may strike it big.

Once the VCs or the PEs come on board, you will lose control and will have to partly share the vision of the investors. Should there be a buyout of your organization at a value less than what the VCs or the PEs put in, your share will come last. There may be a chance you get nothing. A buyout below the current level of valuation will most probably happen only if the market for your product suddenly falls. Just because there is a lot of money in the system, it does not mean you will give up budgetary or fiscal discipline. You will have to exercise it all the more and that is a difficult task. The best way is to steer clear of all external investors and grow organically. Most companies that have grown organically have rarely failed, if their technology or product has not become outdated.

There is a difference between generating money and receiving money. When a business generates money, it becomes sustainable and its valuation will grow. When a business receives large amounts of money from investors due to 'perceived' valuations, the promoter may make money even though the business may not be sustainable.

Debt

Whether it is an individual, organization or a country, debt is something which should be handled with a lot of care. It can spell ruin if it is allowed to go unchecked. There is an easy equation to handle debt. When you are new in the business, keep your debt as small as possible. When you are a mature business, increase your debt, but let it not become too big. When you incur debt, you also have to pay interest. If you cannot pay the interest, it adds on to your principal and balloons your interest cost further. People have been known to have got themselves in a situation where they can only service the interest and not the principal because of indiscriminate use of credit. Both an organization and an individual have to learn to live within their means. As the environment becomes more and more uncertain, debt on your books will be dangerous. Top companies, whose shares dominate exchanges, have relatively less debt than the others that trail behind. All companies that did not have adequate cash reserves went under during COVID-19. Big or small, only businesses that had cash reserves survived probably one of the worst economic disasters of our lifetime. If you must take a debt, it should be to build assets that guarantee returns or security. A good example of this is a house. Buy a house that you will live in or rent out and pay debt and interest comfortably. It is not advisable to buy a car or any white good on debt. Yes, at the idea stage, if you are convinced that your business has a future, take debt but have a plan as to what will happen if events do not go as per plan.

To summarise, debt is like fire, which when small and controllable will warm you and cook your food but if it is raging and out of control, it will destroy you and all those around you.

Valuations

A senior person in the organization told a new entrant in the finance department that he should learn to predict the movement of currencies. He was naïve and today after years of experience, he knows it is exceedingly difficult to predict the future, leave alone the movement of currencies. If we can get the prediction of the future right, even 60% of the time, we would be among the richest in the world. Banks try to do that, but unlike individuals, they have a huge net to fall on, in case predictions go wrong. The way you value a business is by adding up all the cash flows that you think the business will generate in the next five, ten or twenty years. Rarely has it been seen that a projection for big projects has worked out right.

How do you value a new-born baby? After all, isn't a start-up just that? Can anyone say what this baby will earn in his or her lifetime? Do not throw your hands up and say it is impossible. Remember, when you take a loan to buy your house (wise) or a car (unwise), the bank does an assessment that in the future, you will pay your EMIs and the bank will make money on your loan. Let us discuss how some background information can help us make a better prediction.

Remember life and future predictions are about probability and not about certainty. Nothing is certain except death and taxes. However, there are a lot of things that will probably happen.

Valuation is an art not a science. But we can try to make things as scientific as possible.

Valuation of a new-born baby: Let us see what can help us predict the earnings.

1. Country of birth – If the baby is born in a developed country versus a developing country, the chances are the

baby will have a higher income. In USA, per capita income is USD 54,000 whereas in India, the per capita income is USD 2,000. So, just by looking at the country of birth, we have come to an assessment.

2. Family of birth – If the family that the child in India is born in, earns USD 100,000 but the child born in USA is born in a family that earns USD 60,000, you should pause and think. Statistics show that in most cases, the child earns at least as much as other individuals in its family. This has been published in 'The Guardian', based on a detailed study in eleven countries.

Based on the above two parameters, we can roughly estimate the income of the child. It is not as impossible as we thought it was. As the child grows, his or her school grades, aptitude and the country's economy will all play a role in deciding how much the child will earn. When the child becomes an adult, the earning potential will become clearer.

Now, let us see whether we can value Ramodhar's firm which was mentioned in the previous chapter. Consider the stage after Ramodhar has invested ₹20 lakhs in his firm. He has reached the seed stage and gone to a venture capitalist after one year. During that one year, Ramodhar's firm had reached an annual turnover of ₹60 lakhs. The venture capitalist wants to value the firm based on the cash flows for the next ten years. He roughly sees the following points and after examining them, he arrives at a cash flow for the next ten years.

- Entry barriers – they are not too high. The cost of machinery is not high nor is the area of the factory big.

- Size of the market – the market size is huge and consists of many players. As of now, no one player is dominating the market.

- Growth of the market – the market is growing by leaps and bounds. The populace has become very health conscious and wants convenient and nutritious breakfast options. The number of women working outside the home has risen exponentially and will continue to increase. This trend is irreversible. Many men too are fixing meals for themselves and the family. A nutritious meal which is easy to cook is very much a current and future need.

- India's economy is also poised to grow at a fast rate. More disposable income will lead to a greater demand for these products.
- Ramodhar's products seem to be doing well. Starting from scratch, with a small capital, a turnover of ₹60 lakhs has been reached. It is likely that Ramodar's profits will increase by 10% definitely, and maybe even more on an annual basis. The VC draws up a table to evaluate the business.

Profits in ₹ crores		
Year	Growth at 10%	Growth at 15%
0	24.00	24.00
1	26.40	27.60
2	29.04	31.74
3	31.94	36.50
4	35.14	41.98
5	38.65	48.27
6	42.52	55.51
7	46.77	63.84
8	51.45	73.42
9	56.59	84.43
10	62.25	97.09

Now the VC has to discount these cash flows. The VC realises that a risk-free return (such as a fixed deposit), pre-tax is 7%. For him to take a risk, the rate of return he expects, is nothing less than 30% pre-tax. So, he discounts these cash flows at 30%. Recall the formula $T_n = T_o(1+r)^n$ where now $r = 0.3$.

Discounted Profits in ₹ crores			
Year	Growth at 10%	Disc. Factor	Disc. Cash Flow
0	24.00	1.0000	24.00
1	26.40	0.7692	20.31
2	29.04	0.5917	17.18
3	31.94	0.4552	14.54
4	35.14	0.3501	12.30
5	38.65	0.2693	10.41
6	42.52	0.2072	8.81
7	46.77	0.1594	7.45
8	51.45	0.1226	6.31
9	56.59	0.0943	5.34
10	62.25	0.0725	4.52
		Total	131.16

The VC values this business today at ₹131 lakhs. With a 15% growth rate, it will be higher, ₹154 lakhs. The VC is convinced seeing the growth rate, that this is a good business. The VC is confident that the business will grow by 20% seeing the past trend of the food business and the growth rate of the economy. To expand his business, Ramodhar requires ₹80 lakhs. The VC is ready to give this money provided Ramodhar gives him 40% share in the business, with all assets purchased hypothecated to the VC.

In the above illustration, the arithmetic is perfect, as all arithmetic will be. The art is in expecting the estimated cash flows to match reality. In ninety percent of the cases, organizations are overvalued and in ten percent they are undervalued. It is this ten percent who beat the market, make headlines, and inspire everyone else to start a business.

The basic principle of valuation is mainly discounting future cash flows. Market share, market size, entry barriers, technology, world economy, economy of the country, all add up in deciding whether this future cash flow is realistic or not.

A case in point is Educomp, a company which was supposed to revolutionise education in the late 1990s, was listed in the stock exchange, at one point of time, at the price of ₹1100 per share whose face value was ₹10. Its share price is ₹3 today. There are lots of success stories too, and this chapter is aimed not to discourage, but to encourage the entrepreneur, while making everyone aware of how unpredictable valuations can be.

Let us do this exercise for another example, an electric car start-up.

A brilliant automobile engineer decides that he will start a company to manufacture electric cars. How does one value this start-up? There will be about a dozen parameters that have to be considered before the future cash flows can be calculated. As mentioned earlier, projection of future cash flows cannot be accurate but can be done with certain assumptions. This exercise can, at best tell you, whether at this point, there is a chance of profit or there is absolutely no chance of profit. In the early 2000s, an exercise in feasibility of using solar energy was conducted. It clearly showed that solar energy panels were not economical where electricity was available. However, this was twenty years back. Technology has changed so much in these years that now solar energy makes economic sense. Changing technology is a big factor that can make or break businesses. Let us list a few of the parameters that will help predict the future of an electric car start-up.

- Entry barrier in terms of finance and other resources – The higher the entry barrier, the less chance that you will get funding. Today, it is practically next to impossible set up an integrated steel plant. Only governments and big corporates can set up steel plants. A steel plant is highly polluting and water intensive. This is just to clarify that the first point one must check is the entry barrier. The entry barrier for an individual to get into manufacturing electric cars would be formidable. The heart of an electric car is the battery. Would it not make sense for the individual to manufacture the car battery instead of a complete car? Here the entry barrier would be much less.

- Size of the car market today and the percentage of electric cars.
- Growth of this market from the present to the next ten years – this will give an idea of the market size.
- How many established players are there today and what is their market share?
- What superior advantage does this car battery give?
- Assume this car battery gives an advantage no other battery gives, what would be the likely sales and profit?
- We get a value based on the next ten years cash flows.
- How does this value compare with existing players?

I will end this chapter on valuation here. This was simply to give you the idea that valuation, at best is an exercise to indicate whether an organisation will do well in the near future or not. The result is not necessarily the definite outcome and will at most indicate the direction of the profits.

The following pages carry the presentation made to start-up entrepreneurs at IIM Bangalore. It will be a summary as well as a recap of the concepts discussed in this book.

Finance Essentials for Start-Ups

PRADEEP SWAMINATHAN

Introduction

- Accounts is the language of business.
- Money has never been unlimited.
- All of us, in our own ways, account for our money:

a) As students, with limited pocket money or for making demands on our parents.

b) As responsible parents or salaried earners, juggling funds for school fees, household expenses and EMIs.

c) As business owners or executives, trying to make sense of our business.

We Have All Been Accountants

- When the sums were small, we may have addressed the numbers in our minds; money for movies, dinner, books, etc.
- When the sums were big and the transactions numerous, the money spent was accounted for in old diaries or excel sheets.
- There is little difference between managing the accounts of a student, a householder, a small business or a huge corporation.
- If you wish to successfully handle your money, you must know what your money is being spent on.

Accounts And Finance Is A Vast Subject

- I spent three and a half years to earn each of my professional degrees.
- The gap between my two professional degrees was twelve years, and in this decade, much had changed and a lot also remained the same.
- I spent another thirty-six years applying this knowledge.
- I would like to share with you some important concepts that will be most relevant to help you run your business.
- They are easy to understand and I do hope you will apply them.
- When we finish, you may perhaps ask, is this common sense or a part of accounting and finance? You be the judge!

The Concepts That I Deem Important And Essential

1. Capital versus Revenue: What goes to the Profit and Loss account and why? What goes to the Balance Sheet and why?
2. Fixed Cost versus Variable Cost: What is the difference and why is it important?
3. Principle of contribution and marginal costing: What does this principle convey?
4. Cost Reduction: How and where to reduce costs?
5. Balance Sheet: What does it convey?
6. Cash Flows: Importance
7. Amortization of costs: What this means and how it affects the profits of an organization
8. Accounting Standards: What they are and how it might affect you
9. Selling on Credit – Pitfalls
10. The risk when you take debt
11. Valuations
12. What important points are to be conveyed while requesting for funds?

More Equal Among Equals

1. Capital versus Revenue
2. **Fixed Cost versus Variable Cost**
3. **Principle of Contribution and Marginal Costing**
4. Cost Reduction
5. Balance Sheet
6. **Cash Flows**
7. Amortization of costs
8. Accounting Standards
9. **Selling on Credit – Pitfalls**
10. The risk when you take debt
11. Valuations
12. What important points are to be conveyed while requesting for funds?

Capital Expenditure Vs Revenue Expenditure

- There are three statements of accounts
  1. Balance Sheet
  2. Profit and Loss account
  3. Cash Flow statement – contains information from the above two
- Capital Expenditure goes to the Balance Sheet and Revenue Expenditure goes to the Profit and Loss account
- All three statements will be discussed in more detail later on
- The above distinction helps us to analyse the accounts better

Capital Expenditure

- Capital Expenditure involves that expenditure **the benefit of which lasts over a period of time**. The period of time is normally 3+ years. The expenditure involved also is **high** as compared to revenue expenditure

- When we buy a house, we expect that it should last us for our life-time. Similarly, when we buy a car, we expect that it will last us for ten years. TVs, washing machines, furniture, are all examples of capital expenditure in our daily, personal life.

- When we buy a fountain pen, we expect it also to last several years. I know of some friends and family members who have kept their fountain pens going for twenty years and will not dream of using another pen to do something important. Here, since the amount involved is not very high, it is treated as revenue expenditure.

To summarise:

- Expenditure that involves high cash outflow and the benefit of which lasts over a period of time, is capital expenditure.

- This expenditure is **not fully** used to calculate the profit and loss made by an organization.

- Since this expenditure involves a big cash outflow and a long benefit period, start-ups generally should avoid such expenditure when possible.

What Is Depreciation?

- Suppose you buy a dishwasher that costs you ₹1,20,000. This dishwasher will last you for five years. Is it capital or revenue?

- From what little we have studied, it is capital. After five years, the dishwasher will conk out and you have to replace it with a new one.

- A prudent accountant will calculate the expenditure per year. This will come to ₹24,000 (1,20,000÷5). He will charge ₹24,000 each year to the profit and loss account.

- Thus, part of the capital expenditure is charged to the profit and loss account every year depending on the life of the asset.

- This is the concept of depreciation. If you calculate the monthly depreciation, it will be ₹2,000 (24,000÷12). You will see that this monthly depreciation will be similar to the wages that you pay your maid servant for washing the dishes.

- Depreciation is the cost for using your capital equipment for the year.

Revenue Expenditure

- As opposed to capital expenditure, the benefit of revenue expenditure does not last over several years. It may last a month or a year.

- You pay monthly wages to your maid servant to clean your house and utensils. You have to pay her again the next month. The wages that you pay your maid is revenue expenditure.

- Another example of revenue expenditure is rent. The rent that you pay for your flat entitles you to live in that flat for the month. Come next month, and again you have to pay the rent. Similarly, the electricity charges, the water charges, the maintenance charges are all expenditure related to the month.

- Vegetables and groceries are also revenue expenditure.

- To summarise: the benefit of revenue expenditure does not last over a long period and is recurring.

How Does This Impact My Business?

1. You need a place from which you and your team will operate. It could be your father's garage, your study or it could be a place where start-ups are allowed to operate. Now you will have to do a cost-benefit analysis between buying, renting or trying to get a place free.
   - Father's garage – free of cost
   - Your study – free of cost
   - Renting office space in the centre of the city – revenue expenditure, very costly. Unless you get a tangible benefit do not do this.
   - Renting space in the outskirts of the city – revenue expenditure, cheaper than the above option and if you combine residential and office space, may be a good option.
   - **Buying space in the outskirts of the city – capital expenditure, huge cash outflow at the beginning of the project. Is it worth it?**
2. Purchase of computers, software and internet connection
   - Try to purchase a second-hand computer initially. As your business grows you can upgrade it
   - Computer – capital expenditure
   - Software – depending on the type can be capital or revenue; software you buy once but use for many years will be capital, the licence fee you pay every year will be revenue expenditure
   - Internet connection – revenue expenditure

- Mobile Phone – capital expenditure, keep it functional and avoid frills
- Services provider – revenue expenditure

3. Travel Expenditure – revenue expenditure, use online meetings to avoid travel
4. Furniture – capital expenditure, try to get it free or buy second-hand furniture
5. Machinery – if purchased, it is capital expenditure and if rented, revenue expenditure
6. Local travel – Purchasing a car is capital expenditure; renting a vehicle is revenue expenditure

- We all dream of the big bucks. Don't start spending big before you start earning big. Do not be penny wise, pound foolish; don't compromise on quality but try to get value for your money.
- Capital expenditure normally means a long-term commitment. It is best to avoid such expenditure at the beginning of the business as they involve huge outflows of cash.
- Example: You set up a factory with machinery, buildings, etc. If the business goes bust then you are left with assets that you will have to sell dirt cheap. Far better to hire capacity or machinery or a factory building at the initial stages.

Capital Receipts Vs Revenue Receipts

- Capital receipts are not regular and normally happen once in a few years. Revenue receipts are very regular and happen day after day, month after month in an individual or a corporate's life
- Examples of revenue receipts
    1. For an individual – salary, income from property, income from securities
    2. For a corporate – sales, income from property, income from securities
- Examples of capital receipts
    1. For an individual – loan received, sale of a capital asset like property, car, furniture, etc.
    2. For a corporate – proceeds of share issues, loan received, sale of capital assets, etc.

Profit And Loss Account And Balance Sheet

- Profit and Loss account – When revenue receipts and revenue expenditure are set off, you either get a profit or a loss.
- Balance Sheet – When capital expenditure and capital receipts are presented together you get a balance sheet.
- We will discuss the balance sheet in a little more detail later.
- The cash flow statement tries to summarise the above two statements only in terms of cash.
- The profit and loss account along with the balance sheet are prepared on accrual basis.

Fixed Cost Vs Variable Cost

- When you start your business, you will realise that there are costs that are to be incurred irrespective of whether you produce or sell.
- Let us go to the examples we are all best familiar with, our house. Your family pays monthly rent for the house. This is fixed. The rent remains fixed whether you stay there or not.
- The family takes a holiday to Goa. There you stay in a hotel. That cost varies with the number of days you stay at the hotel. The more days you stay, the more you pay. The fewer days you stay, the less you pay.
- Rent is a fixed cost to your family but the hotel cost is variable.
- The electricity at home is variable. The more days you stay at home, the more electricity you consume. It also varies with the season.
- At the hotel, irrespective of how long you use the air conditioner in a day, you do not pay extra for the electricity. The electricity cost is fixed.
- We have two situations: The house rent is fixed and the hotel rent is variable. The electricity cost in your house is variable, but in the hotel, it is fixed.
- In most hotels, when you pay for your room rent, breakfast is included. So, the food, at least as far as breakfast is concerned, is fixed for you. The food you eat at home is variable.
- For the hotel owner on the other hand, electricity and breakfast is variable. The hotel owner pays for the electricity and food depending on the number of units

you have consumed or the number of eggs you have eaten.

- Assuming he is paying rent to the owner of the building, the rent is fixed. So, for you the rent is variable and breakfast and electricity is fixed and for the hotelier the rent he pays is fixed and the electricity and food are variable.
- When expenditure remains constant irrespective of the activity, it is fixed, but when it varies depending on the activity, it is called variable.
- It is not the nature of the cost that makes it fixed or variable but the agreement you enter into, as to how you pay it, that makes it fixed or variable.

Why Is The Concept Of Fixed And Variable Costs Important?

- You are paying an annual rent of ₹1,00,000 for a building in which you manufacture sensors. Let us say the full annual capacity is 1,00,000 sensors.

- If you manufacture 1,00,000 sensors, the cost is ₹1 per sensor (₹1,00,000÷1,00,0000). If you manufacture 50,000 sensors, the cost is ₹2 per sensor. But if you manufacture 20,000 sensors, the cost per sensor is ₹5 (₹1,00,000÷20,000). If you do not manufacture a single sensor, you will still lose ₹1,00,000.

- When the cost is fixed and the output is low, the cost per unit increases. This means that, in case your start-up is not able to market its products well in the initial period, you will be incurring high costs for being idle.

- In the example of the sensor, you buy material for sensors. Let us say, a small chip for ₹30 per chip.

- The chips you will buy depend on the number of sensors you plan to manufacture. If you plan to manufacture 10,000 sensors you will buy only 10,000 chips and pay ₹3,00,000. If you plan to manufacture 5,000 sensors you will buy 5,000 chips and pay ₹1,50,000. Your cost per chip remains ₹30 per chip. So, your variable cost per sensor does not increase or decrease with production.

- The more the activity level, the cheaper per unit the fixed cost (rent) becomes and the less your activity level, the costlier per unit the fixed cost becomes.

- So, logically, if you think early on in your business there is uncertainty, what should most of your costs be? Variable!
- Also, as your business grows and prospers, the attempt should be to make the costs fixed.

Controlling Cash Outflows And Costs

When you start your business, your earnings will be very uncertain. If your costs are mainly fixed, as has been explained, your expenditure will be committed, and if things do not go well, you will be out of cash.

You want a place to start your business from where you either provide a service or manufacture a product

1. Buy land and fabricate a building at the outskirts – this is capital expenditure. The advantage is, after you buy this, there is not much expenditure, but it will involve a huge cash outflow.

    - What is the solution? Can you buy unutilised capacity in a factory? You achieve everything with a much lower cash flow. Pay as you use contract. So, we have avoided a huge cash flow and made our costs linked to production. In effect these costs are variable.

2. Rent premises – a revenue expenditure and a much lower cash flow.

    Disadvantage – it is a fixed cost; whether you manufacture or not, your service generates a cash flow or not, you will pay rent. Your business model may need you to have an outlet at the centre of the city. By all means, rent a floor. Only accept that this is a fixed cost, and you will have to pay the rent irrespective of whether you get any income or not.

3. Shared office space – again revenue expenditure; much cheaper to rent a desk or a couple of desks for those people who have to be visible. The back office can work from a garage or a place at the outskirts or even from their homes.

You require software to run your business – look at open-source software.

One of the most important requisites of any business will be people.

- Remember, the wage cost is always fixed. Whether the business runs or not, the wage you pay is fixed. How does one make this variable without it adversely impacting your business or exploiting your team?

i. Make the wage partly fixed, partly variable and partly based on profits.

ii. Employ people who may be happy to work on an hourly basis. Those who have recently retired bring with them the wealth of experience and will jump at the prospect of doing something challenging. For a majority of them, money is not a criterion. Qualified individuals for whom working from home is a necessity, such as those with infants at home or parents to be looked after.

iii. Outsourcing – employ a firm on an hourly basis to do tasks like accounting, tax, security, housekeeping etc.

Cost-Benefit Analysis: Buy Vs Hire

What are the costs that are connected with buying and using a car?

- Capital Cost: ₹8,00,000
- Useful life of a car: 10 years
- Driver's salary: ₹10,000 per month
- Lifetime maintenance over the useful life: ₹4,00,000
- Insurance and road tax: ₹20,000 per annum
- Petrol at the cost of: ₹73 per litre

➢ We now have to annualise the costs of the car:
  1. Capital Cost = ₹8,00,000
     Life in years = 10
     Sale value at end of 10 years = ₹1,00,000
     Cost to owner = ₹7,00,000
     Annual cost = ₹70,000
  2. Monthly salary of driver = Rs10,000
     Annual salary = ₹1,20,000
     Medical, Bonus etc = ₹20,000
     Annual Cost = ₹1,40,000
  3. Lifetime maintenance = ₹4,00,000
     Annual Cost = ₹40,000
  4. Insurance and Road Tax = ₹20,000/annum

- **The fixed cost = ₹2,70,000 (whether you drive a single km or not)**

In a year, the car is driven 1,00,000 km.

This car gives a mileage of 10km per litre of petrol, so you will buy 10,000 litres, @ ₹73/l

- **The variable cost will be ₹7,30,000**
- **The total cost is ₹10,00,000**

What are the costs in hiring a car?

The cost of hiring a car is ₹14 per km

- **The annual cost is ₹14,00,000, if you are travelling 1,00,000 km in an annum**
- **Annual cost of hiring a car is ₹14,00,000 vs buying which is ₹10,00,00**

➤ Looking at it on a purely cost basis, it makes sense to buy a car, if you are travelling 1,00,000 km in an annum.

➤ If you are travelling 50,000 km in a year, does it make economic sense to buy a car?

For buying a car:

Fixed cost will not change = ₹2,70,000

Variable cost (petrol @ ₹73/l for 50,000 litres) = ₹3,65,000

- **Total cost of buying a car = ₹6,35,000**
- **Annual cost of hiring a car = ₹7,00,000**

It can be clearly seen that as the kilometres reduce, the cost of hiring a car becomes more economical. This is because of the role of fixed costs.

- When does it break even?

The equation below will answer that question.

2,70,000 (fixed cost) + 7.3 (variable cost of petrol/km) x no. of km = 14 (cost of hiring/km) x no. of km

2,70,000 = 6.7 x no. of km

No. of km = 40,398

Below this, it makes sense to hire a car; above this, it makes sense to buy a car.

➤ Following this method, a simple calculation helps to make a decision regarding buying or hiring.

Marginal Costing

Marginal costing helps us to make decisions regarding:
- How much to produce
- What quantities we should sell
- At what price we should sell
- How to avoid making a loss

Marginal cost is the variable cost of a product or a service.

We have discussed the concept of fixed and variable cost earlier.

Fixed cost does not change with the output of an organization whereas variable cost varies with the output.

Contribution

Selling price is the price we charge to the customer for which he pays us money.

- Please note, it is not the list price. It is the price for which the customer gives you money. In some cases, the list price and the selling price can be the same. Where there is a discount over the list price, the selling price will be the price after the discount.
- Usually where there are products that are to be sold, it is the selling price per product.
- Where it is a service, it is the selling price per hour, per day, per month or per year.
- **Contribution per unit sold = selling price per unit – marginal cost (variable cost) per unit**

Factory Making Pashmina Shawls

We have set up a small factory where Pashmina shawls are made.

- Four craftsmen have been employed and they are paid on the basis of output. For each shawl they are given ₹10,000.
- The material for the shawl including the thread and other accessories is ₹15,000 per shawl.
- As part of the contract with the workers, the workers are provided with accommodation and food. Part of the space where they are accommodated is utilised exclusively as a shopfloor for manufacture of the shawls. The rent for their accommodation and shopfloor comes to ₹60,000 per month.
- The four workers are able to manufacture 20 shawls per month.
- Depending on the month, the number of shawls sold varies along with the price.
- You have a discussion with your accountant regarding each month.
- The best period is the quarter October to December. You get a price of ₹40,000 per shawl. You can sell 60 shawls.
- The next best season is January to March. The price falls to ₹35,000 per shawl but you are able to sell 60 shawls.
- The season April to June is the worst. You can sell only 40 shawls at ₹20,000 per shawl.
- The season July to August is marginally better. You can sell 40 shawls at ₹27,000 per shawl.
- Your accountant gives you the following calculations. You modify them a bit and you arrive at a decision.

Factory Making Pashmina Shawls: October To December

- Number of shawls made = 60
- Income at ₹40,000 per shawl = ₹24,00,000
- Marginal or Variable cost per shawl Labour = ₹10,000, Material = ₹15,000; Total = ₹25,000
- Variable cost of 60 shawls = ₹15,00,000
- Contribution = ₹9,00,000
- Note Contribution is not your profit. We have yet to deduct the fixed costs.
- Fixed Cost is ₹60,000 per month.
- Fixed cost for the quarter is ₹1,80,000
- Profit = Contribution − Fixed Cost

  = ₹9,00,000 − ₹1,80,000

  = ₹7,20,000

➢ When the organization does well, there is no necessity for deep analysis.

Factory Making Pashmina Shawls: January To March

- Number of shawls made = 60
- Income at ₹35,000 per shawl = ₹21,00,000
- Marginal or Variable cost per shawl Labour = ₹10,000, Material = ₹15,000; Total = ₹25,000
- Variable cost of 60 shawls = ₹15,00,000
- Contribution = ₹6,00,000
- Note Contribution is not your profit. We have yet to deduct the fixed costs.
- Fixed Cost is ₹60,000 per month.
- Fixed cost for the quarter is ₹1,80,000
- Profit = Contribution – Fixed Cost

  = ₹6,00,000 – ₹1,80,000

  = ₹4,20,000

➢ When the organization does well, there is no necessity for deep analysis.

Factory Making Pashmina Shawls: July To September

- Number of shawls made = 40
- Income at ₹27,000 per shawl = ₹10,80,000
- Marginal or Variable cost per shawl Labour = ₹10,000, Material = ₹15,000; Total = ₹25,000
- Variable cost of 40 shawls = ₹10,00,000
- Contribution = ₹80,000
- Note Contribution is not your profit. We have yet to deduct the fixed costs.
- Fixed Cost is ₹60,000 per month.
- Fixed cost for the quarter is ₹1,80,000
- Profit = Contribution − Fixed Cost

  = ₹80,000 − ₹1,80,000

  = −₹1,00,000

> The organization is making a loss, there is now a necessity for analysis.

- What are your options?
  - Close down manufacture – you lose ₹2,60,000 (fixed cost ₹1,80,000 + contribution ₹80,000 that you would have earned)
  - Continue manufacture – you lose ₹1,00,000 (contribution ₹80,000 that you have earned –fixed cost ₹1,80,000)

Factory Making Pashmina Shawls: April To June – The Worst Season

- Number of shawls made = 40
- Income at ₹20,000 per shawl = ₹8,00,000
- Marginal or Variable cost per shawl Labour = ₹10,000, Material = ₹15,000; Total = ₹25,000
- Variable cost of 40 shawls = ₹10,00,000
- Contribution = –₹2,00,000
- Note Contribution is not your profit. We have yet to deduct the fixed costs.
- Fixed Cost is ₹60,000 per month.
- Fixed cost for the quarter is ₹1,80,000
- Profit = Contribution – Fixed Cost

    = –₹2,00,000 – ₹1,80,000

    = –₹3,80,000

➤ The organization is making a loss, there is now a necessity for deep analysis.
- What are your options?
    - You cannot change the market. So, income is fixed.
    - You are not even able to cover your variable costs. Continuing to manufacture does not help. You will be losing money if you continue to make shawls.
- Possible Strategies:
    - Speak to your workers. Tell them times are bad. If they are ready to cut their labour costs to ₹7,000, you can keep them. You have to tell them that if they are

unwilling to do so, they will have to look for employment elsewhere.

- Similarly, you will have to negotiate with your suppliers. Tell them that you have dropped prices and demand a 20 percent discount. They may agree as for them also it is a matter of survival.

Factory Making Pashmina Shawls: April To June – After Negotiation

- Number of shawls made = 40
- Income at ₹20,000 per shawl = ₹8,00,000
- Marginal or Variable cost per shawl Labour = ₹7,000, Material = ₹12,000; Total = ₹19,000
- Variable cost of 40 shawls = ₹7,60,000
- Contribution = ₹40,000
- Note Contribution is not your profit. We have yet to deduct the fixed costs.
- Fixed Cost is ₹60,000 per month.
- Fixed cost for the quarter is ₹1,80,000
- Profit = Contribution – Fixed Cost
  = ₹40,000 – ₹1,80,000
  = –₹1,40,000

> The organization is still making a loss. Now, some tough decisions have to be taken.

- How can the business be saved? Should you stop the business or continue?
  - The cons of stopping are: restarting is tough, your employees may be poached, the costs may go up when you restart.
  - If you retain the premises, you lose ₹1,80,000.
  - If you continue your business your loss is less, ₹1,40,000.

All this analysis is possible because we have distinguished between fixed and variable cost.

A Business Has Three Scenarios

- Scenario 1: The business makes a profit.
- Scenario 2: The business is able to cover variable costs but not fixed costs. Does it make sense to continue this business? In the long run, with some sound strategies in place to reduce fixed costs, the business should thrive.
- Scenario 3: The business is not able to recover its variable costs. This is a dangerous situation and it really does not make sense to run the business on a long term. Unless the issue of at least covering your variable cost is addressed, it does not make sense in continuing with this business.

Break Even Point

- Contribution – Fixed Cost = Profit
- Breakeven point is that level where profit is zero i.e., where contribution is equal to fixed cost. Above the breakeven point a profit is made, below that, a loss.

In the above example, let us try to capture the breakeven point for the best quarter.

    Contribution = Fixed Cost

    Fixed Cost for the quarter = ₹1,80,000

    Contribution per shawl = selling price – variable cost = ₹40,000 – ₹25,000 = ₹15,000

    ₹15,000 x no. of shawls = ₹1,80,000

    No. of shawls = 12

- So, if we sell more than 12 shawls, we make a profit and below 12, we make a loss.
- Using this simple tool, we get an idea of how much we should sell and at what price. It helps in negotiations and in strategies to reduce cost.

In the same example the distributor tells you that if you reduce the price by ₹10,000 in the peak season per shawl, he will be able to sell a greater number of shawls. What will be the breakeven number? Should you reduce the price?

    Contribution per shawl = selling price – variable cost = ₹30,000 – ₹25,000 = ₹5,000

    ₹5,000 x no. of shawls = ₹1,80,000

    No. of shawls = 36, to break even

Let us say that due to the reduced price, the number of shawls sold jumps from 60 to 150.

Contribution = 150 x ₹5,000 per shawl = ₹7,50,000

Fixed cost is ₹1,80,000

Profit = ₹7,50,000 − ₹1,80,000 = ₹5,70,000, as against ₹7,20,000 earlier.

You have to take a decision whether you want more profits or more volume of sales.

Cost Reduction

Penny wise, pound foolish: This is something to be always kept in mind for reducing costs.

- Example: You buy a sneaker that costs you ₹200 which lasts you for two months. Your neighbour buys a sneaker that costs you ₹1200 which lasts him two years. The shoe you purchased cost you ₹100 per month and the shoe your neighbour purchased cost him ₹50 per month. Prima facie, your neighbour has purchased a cheaper shoe even though it cost him more.
- There are a few twists to the above.
    1. What if in the two years you will wear this only for 60 days and your neighbour will wear it for 600 days? So, usage also counts.
    2. Because the design of the cheaper shoe is bad, there are chances that you will slip and fall and sprain your leg. Doctor's fees may go up to ₹10,000
- Does a higher price mean better quality? No not always.
- The success of the cost saver is getting something much cheaper to perform the same function.
- This is one of the objectives the quality movement is supposed to achieve: Improved performance with simultaneous price reduction.

A Practical Example In Cost Reduction

- I was posted in a malaria prone area. It was very scenic and beautiful but the chance of getting malaria was high.
- The accommodation that we were given was well-ventilated and spacious but there was no mosquito netting on the windows. The local contractor was ready to manufacture windows with netting but the cost was prohibitively high.
- My wife then suggested a product called 'Netlon'. One can tape or nail Velcro around the window. The edges of the net have the clinger and the net can be mounted on the window.
- Hey presto, the same function was achieved at one tenth the cost!
- The only disadvantage was that it took a little longer to remove the net. Now, in this scenario is opening or removing the net important? No! Far better that the net remains there all the time.
- However, if opening and closing the window was frequent and important, then this would not be a good substitute.

Life-Cycle Costing

In short, a cost is just not about the price you pay. There are many factors that you take into account and this type of evaluation is called life-cycle costing.

What is important in life-cycle costing is that we consider:

- Usage
- Convenience
- Affordability
- Maintenance
- Other costs associated with it.
- It also means not to get fooled by brands and to ensure that you get value for money.

An Example In Cost-Benefit Analysis

Sumanth had never taken tuitions in his life. For his CA final exam, he is a little weak in the taxation paper. There is a very good tutor near his house but the tutor is expensive. The tutor charges ₹2000 per month.

- His father tells him that if he qualifies as a CA in his first attempt and starts earning ₹20,000 per month, in six months he will earn ₹1,20,000.
- Whereas, in the six months leading to the exams he will spend only ₹12,000 on the tutor. Moreover, a good tutor will spark an interest and cement his foundations in tax which may lead to him becoming a top-class tax professional.

Somnath listens to his father's advice and aces his tax paper and passes his CA in his first attempt.

Cost-Benefit Analysis – A Sorry Story

In a huge project costing several hundred million USD, the furnace is the most expensive part of the project. Due to safety reasons, the specifications of the furnace stand have to be complied with to the last bolt. Any small deviation and the furnace stand can be rejected by the furnace supplier. If the project owners build the stand, the cost will be USD 150,000. If the furnace suppliers build it, it will be USD 300,000. The cost of the furnace is USD 60 million.

The following are the outcomes if the furnace suppliers reject the furnace stand:

- The project will be delayed by six months
- Six months of production loss translates into a cash loss of USD 10 million

Any sensible CEO will ask the furnace supplier to make the furnace stand. Not this CEO! He thought he would save USD 150,000 and landed up losing USD 10 million.

➢ **Cost Saving is very important but don't forget to see the big picture!**

Cost-Benefit Analysis

We have to be very clear as to what function we wish to carry out. Let us now take an example of a transport agency.

- Transport of goods come in many shapes and sizes. How much do we want to transport at a time? You have big trucks and small trucks. The capacity range is from 0.85 tons to 32 tons.
- Obviously, the cost of a 32-ton truck and trailer will be much more than a 0.85-ton truck. The price ranges from 4 lakhs to 40 lakhs.
- So, there is a close co-relation between price and function.

Let us say, you have decided to be in the small segment. i.e., 0.85 tons

Option A: Brand X

- Capital Cost: ₹4 lakhs
- Life: 10 years
- Maintenance over lifetime: ₹3 lakhs
- Insurance: ₹30,000 per annum
- Cost of Diesel/km: ₹5.5
- Annual mileage: 20,000 km per annum
- Resale value: 0

  Now let us annualise the costs

- Capital cost per annum = ₹40,000
- Maintenance = ₹30,000
- Insurance = ₹30,000

- Mileage costs = ₹1,10,000
- ➢ Annual cost = ₹2,10,000

Option B: Brand Y

- Capital Cost: ₹6 lakhs
- Life: 10 years
- Maintenance over lifetime: ₹2 lakhs
- Insurance: ₹40,000 per annum
- Cost of Diesel/km: ₹4.0
- Annual mileage: 20,000 km per year
- Resale value: 0

  Now let us annualise the costs
- Capital cost per annum = ₹60,000
- Maintenance = ₹20,000
- Insurance = ₹40,000
- Mileage costs = ₹80,000
- ➢ Annual cost = ₹2,00,000

You can see that the biggest single cost is the cost of fuel. Hence, when you do the life-cycle costing, you should take into consideration which truck gives you the best mileage.

Even though option B has the higher capital cost, the life-cycle cost is lower.

If the mileage is more, the difference will be greater.

Balance Sheet – What Does It Convey?

Recap:
- Capital expenditure and capital receipts are presented in the balance sheet
- Capital Expenditure – long-term assets
- Capital Receipts – long-term liabilities

The balance sheet also has:
- Short-term assets created
- Short-term liabilities taken

A balance sheet of an entity conveys what an entity is **worth, at a particular point of time.** The entity can be an individual, an organization or a huge corporate.

- It is very important to understand that the worth is valid **only** as on the date of the balance sheet.
- The worth may change at any time. There may be big developments after that date, that will totally destroy the worth of the individual or increase his worth greatly.

Balance Sheet Of Surya On 31.12.2020

Liability	Value in ₹
Housing Loan from Bank	10,00,000
Loan from friend	2,00,000
Payments due for Insurance policies	1,00,000
Total of liabilities	13,00,000

Asset	Value in ₹
One Flat in Bangalore	80,00,000
Fixed Deposit in SBI	5,00,000
Shares in ITC	10,00,000
Furniture	75,000
White Goods in the House	25,000
Car	4,00,000
Clothes of self and wife	10,000
Jewellery	2,00,000
Retirement Benefits accrued	75,00,000
Insurance Policies	20,00,000
Total of assets	1,97,10,000

Net worth: ₹1,84,10,000

Comments On The Net Worth

To comment on Surya Prakash's net worth, we would also need to know his age.

Let us take three different ages.

1. If Surya Prakash is 33 years old, he has been very successful in amassing this wealth at a young age.
2. If Surya Prakash is 50 years old, then he is moderately successful and he has ten years to increase his net worth.
3. If Surya Prakash is 60 years old, his success is above average but not exceptional.
   - So, when you calculate the net worth of an entity, you should also be prepared to calculate the future earning capacity of the individual.
   - Similarly in a business, given the technology, life-cycle of the product, life-cycle of the industry and other factors, we can assess what its future net worth will be.

Balance Sheet Of Malakar Babu

Liability	Value in ₹
Loan from money lender	2,00,00,000
Housing Loan from Bank	10,00,000
Payments due for Insurance policies	1,00,000
Total of liabilities	2,11,00,000

Asset	Value in ₹
One Flat in Bangalore	80,00,000
Fixed Deposit in SBI	5,00,000
Shares in ITC	10,00,000
Furniture	75,000
White Goods in the House	25,000
Car	4,00,000
Clothes of self and wife	10,000
Jewellery	2,00,000
Retirement Benefits accrued	75,00,000
Insurance Policies	20,00,000
Total of assets	1,97,10,000

Net worth: – ₹13,90,000

Comments On Net Worth

- You will observe that the assets of Malakar Babu and that of Surya are the same.
- The loan that Malakar Babu has taken from a money lender has vitiated his net worth. Malakar Babu had a tip from his doctor friend that there was one medicine that cured COVID-19 and was available. If Mr Malakar Babu could purchase ₹2 crores worth then in the market, it could be sold for three times the cost. Mr Malakar Babu borrowed this money at an annual interest of 25%. The tip provided to be a false lead and both Malakar Babu and his friend are in deep trouble. So, a get-rich-fast scheme has destroyed the net worth of Malakar Babu.
- Malakar Babu's ability to repay the loan will depend on his age and future earnings.
- So, risk taking capacity changes with time. We are not talking about exceptional cases, only a trend.

Cash Cycle Of A Salaried Individual

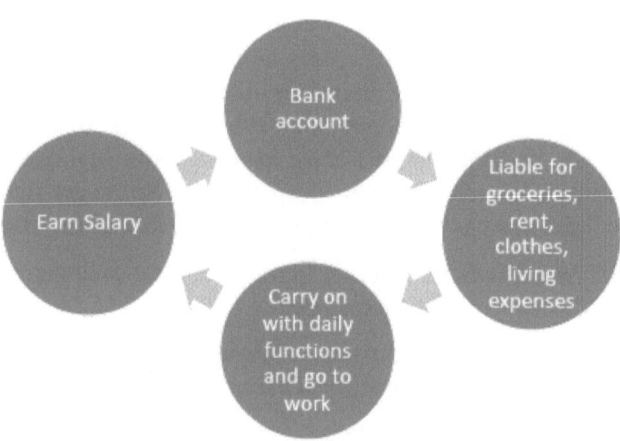

Cash Cycle Of A Salaried Individual

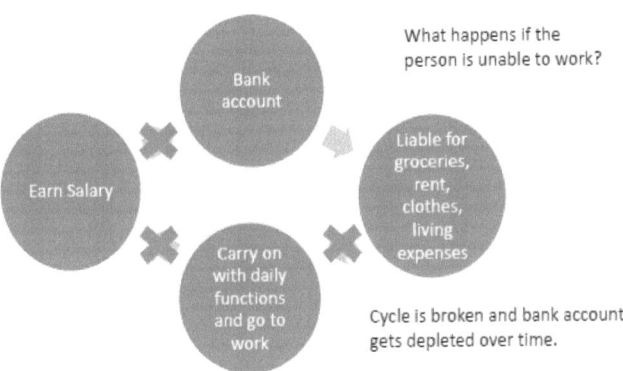

Working Capital Cycle Of A Corporate

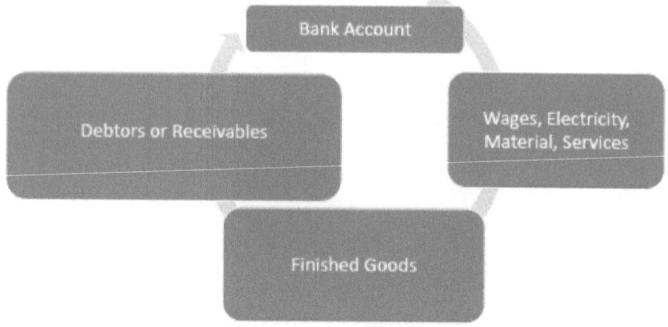

What Are We Trying To Convey?

- You will see in the illustration that the boxes get bigger and bigger. It has been done deliberately. This is because of value addition.
- Your employees' efforts for which you pay them the wages, the electricity for which you pay the municipality and the raw material for which you pay your supplier of goods, all are combined to make a product or a service or a combination of the two, worthy of sale. There is also the cost of depreciation of machinery and buildings and so your finished goods and services are higher in value than the inputs.
- When you sell, you add a mark-up or profit which makes the next box even bigger.
- The faster you convert this cycle, that is, turn your employees' efforts into cash, the more efficient you are.
- When do the boxes spring a leak?
  1. When your employees using the materials are not able to convert the goods for sale. That can happen for many reasons. Sub-standard quality, incorrect pricing, insufficient demand for the goods.
  2. When your marketing team is unable to sell, the finished goods pile up and are unable to convert into the next level.
  3. If your marketing team is not able to realise the money from making the sale, the last leg is incomplete and you do not get cash.
- If the leak is not fixed, you have to borrow more money. Borrowing more money means more interest and less profit. Also, you can borrow more money only up to a point of time. After this, you will run out of credit and money, and will have to close your organisation.

Working Capital Cycle Of A Corporate

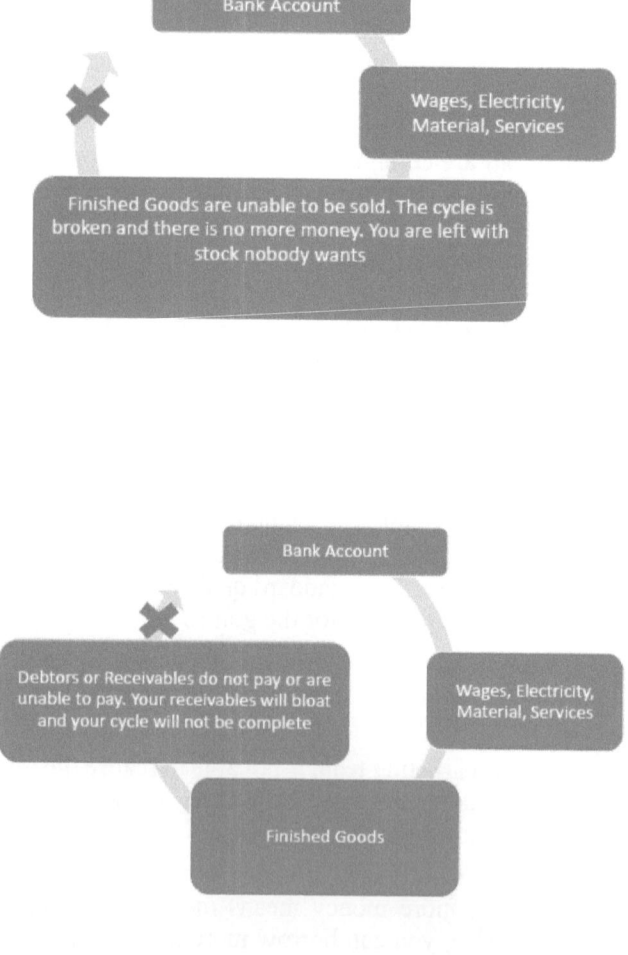

Working Capital Management

In the above examples, it has become very clear what happens when your cash cycle is incomplete.

- You have to continue to pay wages, rent, suppliers of goods and services but, because of either inability to sell finished goods or default of debtors, you do not receive funds.
- If the problem is not sorted out, you will run out of funds.
- In case you continue to borrow money, then you will pay costly interest which will eat into your profits.

Even though the concept is simple, working capital management in most companies is not handled very well.

Some simple calculations:

- If your annual sales are ₹60 crores and your finished stock is ₹20 crores,

    60 crores = 12 months sales

    20 crores = 20/60 x 12 months = 4 months sales

    ₹20 crores, the stock you are carrying is the equivalent of four months sales.

- Why are you carrying stock for a period of four months? It depends on the business, but anything more than six months stock is a red flag.
- In the same example, if your debtors or receivables are ₹40 crores, they are the equivalent of 40/60 x 12 months = 8 months.
- In Debtors, anything over 3 months sales is considered very inefficient; and in some cases, you have to disclose

to your shareholders the debtors which is more than six months sales.

➢ In effect, your customer, instead of borrowing from the bank, is financing his business by not paying you on time.

- Do not think that you can reduce your borrowings by not paying your employees and suppliers on time.
- If your customers don't pay and there is no money in your top box (bank), you may think that you can defer paying your employees and suppliers. There are consequences:
  1. Legislation demands that you pay your workers on time. Also, not paying your workers will mean shrinkage in employee morale.
  2. Some utilities that supply water and electricity will shut off your electricity and water if you do not pay.
  3. Not paying your suppliers on time will destroy their working capital cycle too. Over a period of time, you will get the reputation of being an irresponsible provider and either your suppliers will not provide goods or services or will increase the prices.
- **Cash management, especially working capital management, is a very important part of your business, more so for start-ups.**
- Imagine you have purchased a top of the range car. It has got the best features possible. One day, while driving, you run out of petrol. This wonderful car with all its features is now useless, because you did not pay attention to the petrol gauge. What petrol is to the car, cash is to your business. If you do not monitor your stock levels and debtors (very similar to not looking at the gauge), you will run out of cash and your business with very high potential will come to a stop.

- On a lighter side, if you have convinced a provider of finance to permit you to burn cash, you can continue to handle your business inefficiently.

Balance Sheet Of A Corporate

We have already discussed that the balance sheet of any entity is the difference between the sum of its assets and the liabilities it owes. What we have discussed earlier is once again reproduced below.

A balance sheet of an entity conveys what an entity is **worth, at a particular point of time.** The entity can be an individual, an organization or a huge corporate.

- It is very important to understand that the worth is valid **only** as on the date of the balance sheet.
- The worth may change at any time. There may be big developments after that date, that will totally destroy the worth of the individual/organization or increase the worth greatly.

In the case of a corporate or organization, even though the fundamental principle remains the same, there are a few small issues which will be made clear.

- In a corporate, the assets and liabilities are divided into long-term and current. Normally, those which last over more than a year are long-term and those that last less than a year are current.
- To recapitulate, expenditure whose benefit lasts more than a year goes to capital and that which is less than a year is revenue.
- What will be our short-term assets? In the working capital cycle, stock and debtors will be current assets.
- Revenue expenditure – the salary that you pay, the payment for electricity, the payment that you make for operations and marketing, all result in the creation of

your short-term assets. The expenditures that you charge to your Profit and Loss Account result in the creation of your short-term assets.

- Long-term assets normally arise out of capital expenditure and short-term assets arise out of revenue expenditure.
- What will be a corporate's liabilities? The long-term liabilities will be loans that are to be repaid after more than a year. Current liabilities are those that are in the first box of the working capital cycle – liabilities that you have to settle towards your suppliers, employees and utility providers.
- The difference between Current Assets and Current Liabilities is called Working Capital.

Working Capital Cycle Of A Corporate Current Assets And Current Liabilities

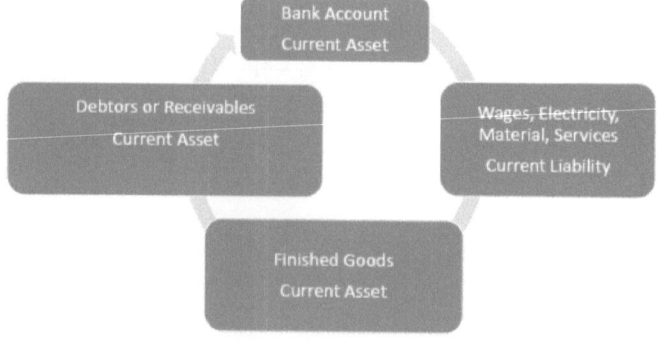

Provision

- Let us say today Shyam's net worth is ₹1 crore. Shyam is a 35-year-old individual, married with one 2-year-old child.
- Can Shyam splurge and buy a Mercedes? Debatable point. Some may say, "Yes, what is the point saving for tomorrow, live life today." Someone who is more serious and conservative would like Shyam to keep money aside for the child's higher education.
- If Shyam has to provide for a child's higher education, the sum that he has to set aside would be ₹50 lakhs. So, Shyam's worth falls down to ₹50 lakhs because of the provision.
- Corporates have to account for many such provisions. For example, there is a lawsuit which the corporate is fighting. The judgement has not been made, but the lawyers feel in all probability, the company will lose ₹50 crores. So, a provision has to be made and depending on when the court will decide, it can be short-term or long-term.

Balance Sheet Of XYZ Ltd.

Assets	Value in ₹
Long term Assets	
Land and Buildings	25,00,000
Plant and Machinery	45,00,000
Current Assets	
Stock	15,00,000
Debtors	10,00,000
Total of assets	95,00,000

Liability	Value in ₹
Long term Liabilities	
Long term Loans	30,00,000
Current Liabilities	
Suppliers	10,00,000
Utilities	5,00,000
Employees	2,00,000
Total of liabilities	47,00,000

Net worth = Assets – Liabilities = ₹48,00,000.00

Net Worth Of An Entity

- Thankfully, you do not have to do this laborious calculation to find the net worth of an audited entity. The difference between the assets and the liabilities is given under the head **'Shareholders' Funds or Owner's Funds'**
- When you divide Shareholders' Funds by the number of shares you get the book value of the share. Normally, the market value is more than the book value of a share
- When the book value is more than the market value, examine the credentials of the promoters and the type of business. If they are good and the business has potential, think of buying those shares.

Book Value

- I have done this exercise for one listed company that I have picked at random.

  Proctor and Gamble Health Ltd
- The Shareholders' funds are ₹816.81 crores as on 31.12.2019
- The number of shares is 1.66 crores
- The book value per share is ₹816.81÷1.66 that is ₹492 per share, the net worth per share
- The share is trading at a market value of ten times its book value, that is close to ₹5,000 per share
- The market perceives that this share has got a great future. Part of the price the market is willing to pay is because of the future growth of Proctor and Gamble. This difference between the book value and the market value can be the subject of a doctorate and is not going to be covered in this book.

Cash Flows

- One of the skills that is very important in running a business is to understand cash flows.
- Let us say you are looking for a prospective business partner. You have a fantastic business idea but you need someone to help finance the business. However, you would like to know the credentials of the person you are planning to do business with.
- One person tells you that he will meet you in a posh restaurant. The person arrives in a chauffeur driven Mercedes and discusses the plan with you over dinner. You are taken up by him and agree to team up with him.
- You consult your financially savvy friend who tells you that the best way to assess his financial strength is to see his bank balance.
- When you see his bank balance, you are in for a shock as you find out that this person does not have much money to his name and had hired a Mercedes and chauffeur for a few hours to impress you.

Importance Of Cash Flows

- The lesson is that all numbers can be tweaked or misrepresented except cash or bank balance. It can also very easily be verified.
- A cash flow statement reveals exactly from where the money has come and how it has been spent.
- It tells you how well or badly a business has performed.
- If you have grasped working capital management, you have grasped eighty to ninety percent of the skill of cash flows.
- The cash or bank balance or its equivalent is one of the important criteria for determining the financial health of an individual or organization.

Cash Flow Of Individuals

Cash flow of Kalyan, studying in Loyola College, a 2nd year BCom student, for the month of November 2020. Kalyan is the son of a middle-class government officer. He lives the high life leading many of his college mates to think he is the son of a rich man.

Source of funds	Value in ₹
Pocket money from father	1000
Loan from Guru	500
Loan from Saurav	500
Total of inflows	2000

Utilization	Value in ₹
Cigarettes	200
Pub	600
Dinner with girlfriend	600
Payment of part loan to Raju	300
Payment of part loan to Ram	300
Total of outflows	2000

The Cash Flow Story

- The first red flag is that against a pocket money of ₹1000, Kalyan is spending ₹2000. He is leading a high life, visiting pubs, smoking and dining with his girlfriend.
- Part of his loan money of ₹1000 has gone to repay loans to other people from whom he had borrowed money. From this statement we can draw a conclusion that four students are involved in lending him money. There may be others who have lent him money before but have not been repaid as yet but we do not know this as the cash flow is for one month.
- Against a sum of ₹1000 of pocket money, he is spending ₹1400, burning a hole of ₹400 in his pocket. If he does this regularly, his debt would increase. His father can barely afford to send him ₹1000.
- So, one can see what a simple cash flow statement can convey about an individual.

Some Cash Flow Rules

When your stock or debtors increase, is it cash inflow or outflow?

- An increase of debtors and stock represents an outflow of cash. A decrease of debtors or stock represents a cash inflow. For a shopkeeper, increase in number of shirts (stock) only happens if he has spent money to buy them. Similarly, decrease in shirts means that he has sold them and he has got money.
- A profit means money has come in and it represents an inflow.
- Increase of borrowings means inflows. You borrow money, your cash comes in. You repay your loans, cash goes out. A decrease in borrowings means cash outflows.

From the above we come across these generic rules:

1. Increase in assets, current and long-term, means cash outflows.
2. Decrease in assets, current and long-term, means cash inflows.
3. Increase in liabilities, current and long-term, means cash inflows.
4. Decrease in liabilities, current and long-term, means cash outflows.
5. Profit means cash inflow.
6. Loss means cash outflow.

Cash Flow Of A Start-Up – First Year

Inflows	In ₹ crore
Venture capital	2.00
Promoter's equity	0.50
Profit from operations	0.25
Increase in creditors for goods	0.50
Total of inflows	3.25

Outflows	In ₹ crore
Plant and machinery	0.50
Increase in debtors	0.75
Increase in finished stock	1.00
Laptops	0.25
Increase in purchased stock	0.75
Total of outflows	3.25

- In any business, new or old, cash is king and you have to conserve cash. The COVID-19 epidemic knocked out most businesses mainly because they had not kept a healthy cash reserve.

Cash Flow Story Of A Start-Up

Let us assume the sales for that first year was ₹2 crores.

Recollecting the formula we had discussed, let us convert the debtors to months of sales:

0.75 crores÷2 crores x 12 months = 4.5 months of sales

➢ The first red flag has popped up. We had mentioned that the normal thumb rule is that debtors should not exceed three months.

Now let us analyse this further. How old are the debtors?

- The sales manager tells you that ₹0.50 cores of debtors is because of a sale that took place during the previous month and ₹0.25 crores is over six months old.
- There has been no follow up because they were busy trying to meet the sales target. Now one can safely say that the ₹0.25 crores is in jeopardy.
- You have to tell your sales team that making a sale is not enough but that one must also collect the cash to complete the sales cycle.

Similarly let us examine the finished stock. The finished stock has gone up by ₹1 crore.

Using the same logic, 1crore÷2 crore x 12 months = 6 months. This means that the finished stock is the equivalent of six months.

➢ Why have we blocked up our money in producing six months stock?

- Your sales team stated that in the next six months because of COVID-19, more than two months stock cannot be sold. You then have to take a call to stop production to liquidate stock.

- The labour will be idle. You can perhaps negotiate for half pay. It may have been best for you to have hired capacity in an already manufacturing unit.

- Now another familiar concept should strike you. If you have started your own production unit, your labour will be fixed cost but when you hire capacity in another unit, it becomes variable.

➤ One more point we must consider is that in our sources of funds, by not paying our creditors we are funding our outflows. We may lose our goodwill and suppliers may not give us credit any more. These are important issues that we should examine and check for how long we have not paid our creditors.

Valuation Of Future Cash Flows

Does money have a time value?

You have a very rich uncle. He is fond of you and gives you the following options:

- Option 1: He will give you ₹5 lakhs tomorrow
- Option 2: He will give you ₹5 lakhs after one year
- Option 3: He will give you ₹5 lakhs after three years.

Which should you choose?

- If you exercise Option 1, you are worried that you will spend the entire money at once. You don't wish to receive ₹5 lakhs now.
- What about Option 2 or Option 3?
- Option 3 is five years away. You and your uncle may not be on the same terms as now.
- Option 2 is a safer option. You will get this money in a year. By that time, you can take a good decision on how to utilise the money. You will not fritter it away.
- You discuss this with your financially savvy friend and he tells you, take this money right away and invest it at once in the post office. He tells you that after one year, before tax, you will get ₹5,35,000 and after five years you will get ₹7,00,000, assuming the rate of interest is seven percent. You are surprised that such a risk-free return is giving you so much money.
- So, money never remains static unless you have stuffed it in your mattress or your pillow cover. There too, money will not be static because it can be stolen or can be eaten by termites.

- When money has a time value and you do your calculations based on this time value, it is called discounted cash flow.

Compound Interest And Opportunity Cost

Let us assume that your uncle gives you the ₹5 lakhs tomorrow and you decide to start your own business.

- You sit with your friend and do some calculations. The worth of your business after one year is ₹5,10,000 and after five years is ₹6,00,000. Does it make sense to take a risky business venture? Shouldn't you put it in the post office as a deposit instead?
- If you want adventure, then join an adventure sport and invest your money in the post office. To do business, you have to be ready to take an informed financial risk.
- To understand discounted cash flow, one has to appreciate the wonders of compound interest.
- Compound interest works exponentially. Don't get taken in by stories of those who make a quick buck. For every one individual who makes a quick buck, there are many hundreds who lose it even faster.
- **Albert Einstein** is reputed to have said, "Compound interest is the eighth wonder of the world. He who understands it, earns it; he who doesn't, pays it."

You start with ₹10 lakhs which you have been gifted and decide to invest this in a bank deposit where the interest rate is 7%.

At the end of the first year, ignoring taxes, the money you have invested will become ₹10.70 lakhs.

Initial sum is ₹10 lakhs

Rate of interest = 7% = 7/100 = 0.07

Interest for one year at 7% is 0.07 x 10 lakhs = 0.70 lakhs

So, the principal plus interest will be ₹10.70 lakhs

This can be put as: $10 (1+.70)^1$

At the end of the second year it will be $10(1+0.70) (1+0.70) = 10 (1.70)^2$

We start off at year 0 (now)

- At year 0 → $10(1+0.07)^0$ = 10 lakhs
- At year 1 → $10(1+0.07)^1$ = 10.70 lakhs
- At year 2 → $10(1+0.07)^2$ = 11.45 lakhs
- At year 3 → $10(1+0.07)^3$ = 12.25 lakhs
- At year 7 → $10(1+.0.07)^7$ = 16.06 lakhs
- At year 10 → $10(1+0.07)^{10}$ = 19.67 lakhs

Just by keeping it in the bank for 10 years, your money has doubled

- At year 20 → $10(1+0.07)^{20}$ = 38.69 lakhs

In another 10 years your money has increased to approximately 4 times

- At year 30 → $10(1+0.07)^{30}$ = 76.12 lakhs

In another 10 years your money has increased to about 7 times

- At year 40 → $10(1+0.07)^{40}$ = 149.74 lakhs

- Let us say instead of ₹10 lakhs you had invested ₹1 crore; at the end of 40 years, your money would have become ₹15 crores.
- Nobody can see the future, but there have been people who have made much more money by investing in businesses or in the stock exchange or in property or in gold. There have been many more people who have lost whatever they had by investing in the above entities.
- So, one has to do one's homework well and invest wisely.
- What does all this have to do with discounted cash flows?

Discounted Cash Flows

- We have seen that ₹10 lakhs invested in 40 years becomes ₹149.74 lakhs
- Let us put it in a form like this:
  $$149.74 = 10(1+0.07)^{40}$$
- Let us make this universal,
  $$T_n = T_o(1+r)^n$$
  T_n being the sum after n years
  T_o being the sum initially invested
  r being the rate of interest that your money should fetch you
- To make our multiplication and calculations easy, let us come up with a formula.
  If after 1 year, we want ₹1, at 7% rate of interest, what should be the money that we should invest today?
  $T_n = 1$
  $r = 0.07$
  $n = 1$
  $\Rightarrow 1 = T_o(1.07)1$
  $T_o = 1 \div 1.07 = 0.935$
- So, if we invest ₹0.935 today, at the rate of 7%, we will get ₹1 at the end of one year.
- Assuming that there is a safe risk-free opportunity, the money of ₹1 at the end of one year is the equivalent of ₹0.935 today.
- So, when you receive ₹50,000 after one year, the present value of that money is 50,000 x 0.935 = ₹46,500

Present Value Of Future Cash Flows

- When you multiply the amount by 0.935 you reduce or discount the cash flow and hence the term, **discounted cash flows.**
- We can prepare the present value tables for five years at 7% rate of interest. (In this example, we are using 7% because here we have a choice of investing this money at this rate in a fixed deposit, which is risk free.)

  $T_n = T_o(1+r)n$

- So, ₹1 after one year will mean you will invest ₹0.935 today

  $1 = T_o (1+0.07)1$

  $T_o = 1/1.07 = 0.935$

- ₹1 after two years will mean you will invest 0.87 today

  $1 = T_o (1+0.07)^2$

  $T_o = 1/1.145 = 0.87$

- ₹1 after three years will mean you will invest ₹0.82 today
- ₹1 after four years will mean you will invest ₹0.76 today
- ₹1 after five years will mean you will invest ₹0.71 today

You have a choice between buying a washing machine and paying a maid. Let us assume that the washing machine and the maid use the same amount of detergent and that electricity costs of the house are reimbursed to you by your company.

So, it only boils down to the capital cost of the washing machine and the salary you pay the maid servant.

Year	Pay out if washing machine bought ₹	Pay out if maid is hired ₹	Present value factor	Present value of outflows ₹
0	20,000	4,000	1.000	4,000
1		4,000	0.935	3,738
2		4,000	0.873	3,494
3		4,000	0.816	3,265
4		4,000	0.763	3,052
Total	20,000	20,000		17,459

If you do not consider the opportunity cost of investing your money of ₹20,000 in a fixed deposit at 7%, it makes no difference whether you buy a washing machine or pay ₹4,000 annually to your maid servant.

The moment you consider the present value of paying your maid versus buying a washing machine, it makes sense to invest your money in a bank deposit and pay your maid servant and not buy a washing machine.

Amortization Of Costs

- In today's world, everything is dynamic. Nothing stays still over time.
- There will be a big difference between when you start your business and a year later. Your balance sheet will change on a day-to-day basis.
- There will be money that you have paid for some asset, for which you expect to get a benefit over five years. Let us say you buy a license fee for a software that is valid for a period of five years. The payment is ₹1,00,000. The expenditure is capital i.e., it will go to the Balance Sheet. This benefit will last over five years, so we will expense ₹20,000 to the Profit and Loss Account each year. This is an example of amortization of costs.
- Let us say after one year, the software has become outdated. You will then expense this entire ₹80,000 to the Profit and Loss account.
- So, the lesson is, when you start your business, in the early days, try best not to create assets that last over a year.
- Try to see that your costs are variable and not fixed at the beginning. Looking at it through another lens, try to avoid capital costs and sizeable cash flows in the early days.

Accounting Standards

- If you see the stock exchange, there are diverse businesses. Their shares trade on a common platform. The stock exchange prices a share on many parameters: Profits, Long-term growth, Return on Investments, Stability of the organization, ...

- There are many more parameters but a majority of them can be seen from the statements of accounts. The statements of accounts have to be uniform. If each organization decides to prepare them on a different set of assumptions, then comparison becomes difficult.

- So that there is uniformity in preparing them, we have accounting standards. Today, in different countries the accounting standards are different. There is an attempt being made to make a uniform accounting standard across the world.

- The Indian accounting standards ensure that the audited accounts prepared in India have uniform accounting rules.

Selling On Credit – Pitfalls

- This is the second most important concept, the working capital cycle being the most important. The concept is simple.
- Think back to your college days. Many of us may have experienced one of these:
✓ Lent money to someone and not got it back
✓ Borrowed money from someone and not repaid it
- In the working capital cycle, if you recollect the receivables box, where your customers do not pay, your working capital cycle suffers.
- In the example above, the money you would have lost would have been small. In your business, say your first sale is ₹5 lakhs and your customer does not pay. What do you do? File a lawsuit? The lawsuit may cost more than the amount to be recovered, not to mention the time lost. If your profit is ₹50,000 on the above transaction, then the profit of ten such transactions are wiped out.
- It is very important that you get your money back every time you sell.
- **How do you ensure this?**

How Do You Ensure You Get Money For Your Products Or Services?

Your bank can play a big role in this and we will discuss the major safety nets that we can put in place to ensure that your customer pays you the money.

1. Letter of Credit: This is the most popular instrument. This is applicable for a big value sale. If you are selling ₹10 lakhs of rice to a customer, in this deal there can be two scenarios:
   i. After the sale takes place, your customer does not pay.
   ii. After the customer gives you the money, you do not supply the goods or you supply sub-standard goods.

   In both cases, it is not a win-win situation.

   - The bank steps in and tells you that if you ship standard goods of quality acceptable to the buyer and give the bank the proof, the bank will pay you the money on behalf of the customer.

   - The bank takes this responsibility and does this act through a letter of credit. The bank also tells the customer that he should give the money to the bank and the bank will ensure that quality goods have been shipped and only after that, will the bank pay the money.

   - The bank will also ask the customer as to who should inspect the goods that are ready for shipment. The same letter of credit ensures that this is done.

   - Normally the buyer opens a letter of credit of the approximate value of the goods with their bank and this letter of credit is sent to the seller's bank.

2. Cash against Documents: In this case, the goods are indirectly given to the bank and the bank will not give the goods to the customer until money is received.

   - The pitfall is that if the customer decides not to collect the goods, the bank is stuck with the goods and will charge you money for storage.
   - The trick is to take about 20% advance for this. Now, even if the customer refuses to pay the balance 80%, you can easily sell this at 80% as it will be a steal for another customer. Also, logically the customer will not like to lose the 20% advance paid.

3. In case you have no option but to sell without security as discussed, do a due diligence or assessment of the customer's credit worthiness. Check up with existing vendors if this person honours his creditors. Does he pay on time? Try to find as much as you can about the customer. Make it clear that the second sale will take place on credit only if the money due on the first is completely received.

4. Post-dated cheques: A bounced cheque can send the issuer of the cheque to jail. So even if credit is given, one can to some extent hedge the risk by taking a post-dated cheque.

   - Have a policy with your marketing team as to how much your exposure will be. If you are dealing with the government or with a company of repute, it is unlikely that they will not pay. You can take your invoice to the bank and the bank will give you money against this for which they will charge interest. This is called discounting your invoice.
   - The idea is not to convey that selling on credit is bad but to know the inherent risks associated with selling on credit and how best you can mitigate this.

Financing The Business: Equity And Debt

- How do you finance your start-up? First generation entrepreneurs have often been successful and lack of finance has not stood in their way.

- As compared to even a decade back, financing has become much easier today. Earlier unsuccessful companies drowned in a sea of debt and their promoters had to fight with their backs to the wall. Today, if you have had equity financiers, you can walk away from the disaster only a little bruised. We are restricting this discussion to promoters who have been people of integrity.

- There have been promoters who have been unscrupulous in the past as well. Share capital was raised in Victorian London to convert cobwebs to gold. The shares were oversubscribed! Fame and riches don't sit on the shoulders of every entrepreneur. They are very choosy and will sit on the shoulders of a chosen few.

- Today, financing has moved beyond banks to Venture Capitalists (VC) and Private Equity (PE) players. They lend at high risk to themselves but demand a part of the equity.

The Danger Of Debt

- Whether it is an individual, organization or a country, debt is something which should be handled with a lot of care. It can spell ruin for any of the three if it is allowed to go unchecked.
- There is a very easy solution to this. When you are new in the business, keep your debt as small as possible.
- When you are a mature business, increase your debt but do not let it get too big. When you incur debt, you also have to pay interest. If you cannot pay your interest, it adds on to your principal and balloons your interest cost further.
- I personally have known colleagues, who because of credit cards have got themselves in a situation where they can only service the interest and not the principal.
- Both an organization and an individual have to learn to live within their means. As the environment becomes more and more uncertain, debt on your books means it is going to be dangerous.

The Danger Of Debt

1. Companies whose shares dominate exchanges, have relatively less debt than the others that trail behind.
2. All companies that did not have adequate cash reserves went under because of COVID-19. Big or small, only businesses that had cash reserves survived probably one of the worst economic disasters of our lifetime.
3. If you have to take a debt, it should be to build assets that guarantee returns or security. Perfect example of this is a house. Buy a house that you will live in and pay debt and interest comfortably.
4. There is no need to buy a car or any white good on debt.
5. Yes, at the idea stage, if you are convinced that your business has a future, take debt, but have a plan as to what will happen if events do not go as envisaged.

> **To summarise, debt is like fire, if it is small and controllable, it will warm you and cook your food. If it is raging and out of control, it will destroy you and all those around you.**

Additional Topics Covered

- How to calculate cost of goods and services sold
- Projecting the Profit and Loss Account
- Projecting the cash flow
- Crisis Management

How To Calculate Cost Of Goods & Services Sold

- We all know what is the cost of a good or service. To put it in layman's language – the money it takes to generate this good or service.
- Why is it important?

  If we sell above the cost, we make a profit. If we sell below the cost, we make a loss.
- How do we calculate the cost of a good or service?

  Any good or service has the following elements
  1. Material
  2. Labour
  3. Overheads (expenditure that cannot be directly attributed to the good or service)

We will discuss this by way of an example:

- Mahesh is a brilliant software engineer. During the lockdown, his firm has closed down and Mahesh decides to follow his passion, cooking. Let us help him cost a meal. What are the costs that he should collect and collate, in order to determine the cost of a meal?
  1. Food material costs: rice, dal, vegetables, spices, oil and other ingredients
  2. Fuel: gas and/or electricity
  3. Labour: assume Mahesh does this single-handed, should this be included or not?

  Let us discuss why this should be included or not:

- If included – realistic: correct cost while scaling up, helps comparisons.
- If excluded – opportunity: cheaper than competitors, no job at present.

Is that all?

What about the following?

1. Material to pack the food
2. Cost to deliver the food
3. Use of the house – debatable like salary
4. Use of the equipment to make the food – vessels, stove, etc. Recollect the concept of depreciation.
5. Maid servant, who comes and cleans the house and vessels.
6. Software used to operate the food delivery, developed by Mahesh.
7. Mobile phone charges, including depreciation of mobile.

Here we see a number of costs – fixed, variable and discretionary.

Can we classify the costs as above?

- Food material costs – variable
- Fuel: gas or electricity – variable
- Labour – fixed and discretionary
- Material to pack the food – variable
- Cost to deliver the food – variable
- Use of the house – debatable like salary, fixed and discretionary
- Use of the equipment to make the food: vessels, stove, etc. – fixed and discretionary

- Maid servant who comes and cleans the house and vessels – fixed and discretionary
- Software used to operate the food business – fixed and discretionary
- Mobile phone charges including depreciation of mobile – fixed and discretionary

How To Calculate Cost Of Goods & Services Sold

Why are we classifying costs as variable, fixed and discretionary?

We will debate by using some numbers and they will be presented below.

- This differentiation will help in pricing a meal.
- Remember the selling price that you quote to a customer has a wide perspective, from the perceived value of the customer to the price your competitor quotes.
- You have to quote that minimum price that will at least generate some additional cash.
- You cannot run a business in which you are continuously going to lose cash.

Can we quantify the costs mentioned earlier?

- Food material costs – variable – ₹50
- Fuel: gas or electricity – variable – ₹5
- Labour – fixed and discretionary
- Material to pack the food – variable – ₹5
- Cost to deliver the food – variable – ₹10
- Use of the house – debatable like salary, fixed and discretionary
- Use of the equipment to make the food: vessels, stove, etc. – fixed and discretionary

- Maid servant who comes and cleans the house and vessels – fixed and discretionary
- Software used to operate the food business – fixed and discretionary
- Mobile phone charges including depreciation of mobile – fixed and discretionary

The variable cost is ₹70. This cost is the additional money that is going out of Mahesh's pocket.

The discretionary and fixed costs are those for which no additional money is going from Mahesh's pocket.

So, if Mahesh sells each food packet for ₹80, he makes a profit of ₹10.

Does he make a book profit? No, because if the fixed and discretionary costs are included, it will exceed ₹80.

➢ We now have set the base for projecting a Profit and Loss account.

Projecting A Profit And Loss Account

- An entrepreneur, however small the business is, has a life far tougher than a CEO of any fortune 500 company. The margins of error allowed are far smaller and even a small error can be a matter of life and death for an entrepreneur.
- Broadly there are two approaches – Leap of faith or Minimum platform to operate on.
- Leap of faith – no guaranteed sales.

  Works well where there is a unique proposition, no competition, new discovery, high skill sets.

  DOES NOT WORK WELL WHERE THERE IS EXISTING COMPETITION.
- Minimum platform – SOME GUARANTEED SALES, useful when market is crowded.
- ➢ How is this connected with projecting the Profit and Loss account?

How To Project A Profit And Loss Account

- The first element that we have to project is sales.
- We have to be realistic, do some market study, the size of the market, study the competition, the position of the products and how the value of your product or service will be perceived.
- Try to get a minimum market size:
  1. See if you can get to sell under a famous brand
  2. Get a minimum off-take agreement with a manufacturer
  3. See if you can generate single big orders for target customers
- Once the sales projection is in place, the rest will follow and over several iterations you will be more accurate.
- Remember there can be a 'black swan' situation and prepare for it
- How do you get the sales numbers?
  - ✓ This is more an art than a science
  - ✓ Rarely, in my career, have I seen a perfect projection
  - ✓ The idea is to give you a rough idea where you stand
- The approach that can be followed is scenario planning.
  1. The worst-case scenario
  2. The best-case scenario
  3. The average scenario
- Unless you have guaranteed sales when you start your business, it is very difficult to predict.
- Does that mean I do not predict?

What Should I Try To Predict?

- The most important prediction you have to make is:

  Do you have cash to run your business for the next month, three months, six months, one year?

- Here scenario planning helps in a very big way.
  1. Will you run out of cash in the worst-case, average-case or the best-case?
  2. How much cash do you need to sustain your business?
  3. Have you prepared a cash budget?

- What is your source of funds?
  1. Family money, limited or unlimited
  2. Venture funds
  3. Bank borrowings at a given rate of interest
  4. A combination of the above

- Your sales may be difficult to predict but your expenditure is not.

  This is because you have no control over your potential customers, but you have total control over your expenses.

- Once you get into an agreement for spending money, you are committed. So, try your best to have an escape clause and don't commit to expenditure over long periods of time.

- At the beginning of your start-up journey, as far as possible, try to avoid unnecessary expenditure.

  We discussed earlier that one should try and keep all expenditure variable in the initial stages of the business.

- At this stage, you must distinguish what expenditure is necessary to run your business and what is not.

➤ To summarise, you must know when your cash will run out and prepare for it.

SWOT Analysis

A SWOT analysis will help you to come up with a realistic strategy.

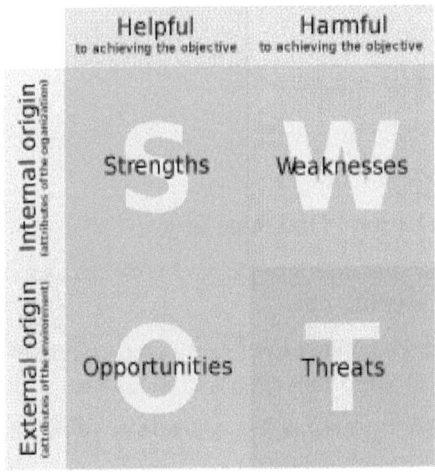

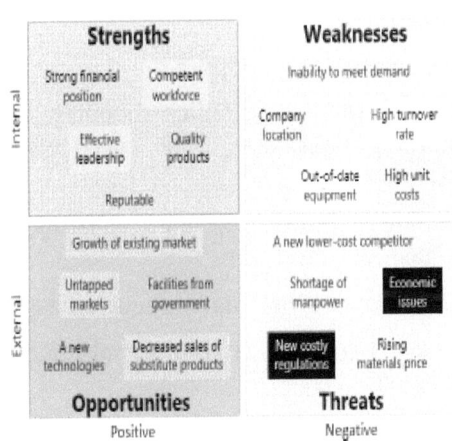

Operating Model

- Today, the business world is flooded with jargons.
- Try to keep your business as simple as possible.
- Obviously, businesses that have:
  - ₹1 lakh turnover
  - ₹10 lakh turnover
  - ₹100 lakh turnover
  - ₹1,000,000,000 turnover

  cannot be run in the same way.
- As your business grows, you will have to relook at the way it is being run.
  - ➢ Are you losing touch with your customer? This is the most important aspect to focus on.

Any organization, small or big, is made up of people, processes and manufacturing technology.

All three are there in different proportions, depending on the type of organization.

- People centric – e.g., hospitality
- Process centric – e.g., online shopping, call centres, outsourcing services like accounts, medical transcription, etc.
- Technology centric – e.g., pharma, hardware manufacturers, steel, etc.

- How do you ensure that this combination delivers value?
- If you have a strategy, is your organization capable of delivering it?

- ➢ Main purpose is to see that the organization is always **customer centric**.

- Historically Tata Steel made mainly longs (bars, channels, rods, …) for the construction industry.
- Over time, Tata Steel also made flats (sheets) for the car, fridge, washing machine industry.
- Customer profile and requirements for the two are different.
- However, for some time the marketing offices sold steel: the same individual would sell both flats and longs. This was not customer centric.
- Subsequently the model had to be changed. The organization was split into two divisions: flats and longs.
- Business structure of the organization was changed in Tata Steel Ltd. to make it more customer centric.
  - ➢ This is a real, live example of how the operation model evolves; What worked yesterday may not work today and what works today may not work tomorrow.

Financial Modelling

- What is financial modelling?

    It is a table that tries to predict the future value of the company. The Financial Model is a table which sets out the future cash flows of the company and assigns these a current value.

- ➢ If your predictions on your sales and expenditure is wrong, your financial model will be totally wrong.

Accounts normally have three statements – Profit and Loss Account, Balance Sheet and Cash Flows. All three are integrated. The normal convention is that the Cash Flow statement is prepared using the Profit and Loss Account and Balance Sheet. Alternatively, the Balance Sheet is prepared using the Profit and Loss account and Cash Flow.

How Do You Value A Start-Up?

- Is it possible to guess how much a new born baby will earn at adulthood?
  - ➢ Forecasting is not about getting everything right; it is about getting most things right. It is about INTELLIGENT GUESS WORK.
- If we do not consider exceptional good luck or bad luck, the geography (where the baby is born) will determine the baby's earning capacity to a large extent. e.g., whether the baby is born in USA, UK, India, Bangladesh, Cameroon, Congo, etc.
- The baby's parents, how rich are they? That will also determine the future earnings of the child.
- As we go along, we come to know the child's grades, conduct, etc. and we can make more educated guesses on the child's future income.

How Do You Value A Start-Up?

Can we apply the same points that we applied to a baby to the start-up?

- Geography – How is the economic environment?
- Business – What kind of activity (trading, manufacturing, service) is the start-up involved in?
- Promoters – Who are the promoters?
- After the business has started how is it performing?

From the above, one can get a rough idea of the value of the start-up.

Financing The Business: What Investors Look At

- Promoter – If the promoter is well known, the chances of getting a bank loan is higher. Thankfully, this is not true for angel investors.

- The standing of the business – New line or expansion? If it is expansion, the chances of getting a loan are better. Angel investors also prefer that you come to them for expansion and not at the very beginning.

- Bankers see if the project is good enough to pay both the interest and the principal. An angel investor wants to see a return of 30%. This means an aggressive top-line and bottom-line growth. The only thing stopping your organization from growing should be lack of funds.

- Bankers want that their loan is secured against assets of the company and, if possible, something more as well. They use a number of methods to safeguard their loans. Angel investors prefer to have a direct stake in the business.

Financing The Business: What Do Angel Investors Look For?

- The three Ts:
  - Traction – simple meaning is grip; does your business have a grip on the market?
  - Team – How good is your team?
  - Target market – How big is the target market?
- Money to expand, not money to start
  - Growth in revenue
  - Growth in profits
- What have you accomplished so far?
- Analytical look at the business
  - What is known?
  - What is unknown?
  - What can be intelligently guessed?

Handling A Crisis

- If you have survived a crisis, you are a success.
- With every crisis there is an opportunity. During the COVID-19 pandemic we suddenly took to online sales, online consultation, online classes.
- You have to adapt and adapt fast. Those organizations that went online survived.
- You have to compromise, not on your principles, but on your fixed ideas. Let us clearly distinguish between value systems and conventions.
- Learn to conserve cash.
  - Spend on essentials
  - Push your creditors
  - Try to get your customers to pay fast
  - Defer discretionary costs
  - Learn to keep a cash reserve for such situations
  - Mothball the business?

What Should Be The Focus Areas Of A Start-Up?

➤ Giving up is not an option.

  Smooth seas do not make good sailors. A failure is a failure only if you give up. When you don't give up, a mistake becomes experience. Change tracks but don't give up.

➤ You should always have cash, so cash forecasting is important.

➤ You have to try to increase your customer base. If your customer base is not growing, you have to find out why.

➤ Are you delivering value? You have to ask yourself this question every minute of the day. If you are delivering value, how can you deliver more?

➤ Do you know your unit economics well? It is initially covering your variable costs, then covering your fixed costs and then making a profit.

THANK YOU!

Also By The Author

Pradeep Swaminathan has written a corporate thriller called 'WHO KILLED THE BOSS'?

Bishal Dev Bandhopadhya was a brilliant individual but a terrible boss. He held a senior position in an organisation of repute in Bangalore. One afternoon, Bishal is found collapsed on his table and dies soon after he is taken to the hospital. His coffee has been laced with poison. Is this murder or suicide?

Prakash Chari resigned from a multi-national to start his own detective agency. In the one year that the detective agency had operated, they were lucky in solving a number of varied cases. This is their first big challenge. Everything seems to point towards suicide, but Prakash and his team are not convinced. Luckily for Prakash, he has a great team: Pramod – a retired police detective, Gautam – an ex-colleague and a great friend, Jayanthi – an attractive software engineer who is also a skilful hacker.

Hardly anyone liked to work under Bishal and on his death, none of his colleagues at the corporate office were sad; on the contrary they seemed to be relieved. As the agency continues its investigation, the pressure is on to close the case as a suicide. When they stumble on the truth, they don't like what they have discovered.

This fast-paced book takes you through the mind of a young detective as he finds himself in the middle of a corporate power struggle where the winner's stake is one of the most profitable companies in India.

The book is highly-rated and available on Amazon and Flipkart.

WHO KILLED THE BOSS?

PRADEEP SWAMINATHAN

Bishal was a tyrannical boss, someone you would not wish on your worst enemy. One day, he collapses in his office and dies very soon after he is taken to the hospital. His morning coffee is laced with poison. Prakash Chari has opened a detective agency, and this will be his team's first major case. Everything seems to point towards suicide, but he and his team are not convinced. This narrative takes you through the mind of a first-time detective as he finds himself in the middle of a corporate power struggle in India. Luckily for Prakash he has a great team: Pramod – a retired police detective, Gautam – an ex-colleague and a great friend, Jayanthi – an attractive software engineer who is very good at hacking. Together they try to piece together this difficult jigsaw and when they do, they don't like what they have discovered.

 Pradeep Swaminathan has had a successful career as a corporate executive. He has held positions on the board of listed companies. In his second innings, he works for an NGO which helps farmers market their produce directly to the consumers.

He discovered the joy of story-telling while narrating bedtime tales to his children. His articles have been published in the Reader's Digest and The Hindu. His first book was privately circulated and was given a good review by The Hindu. This book is the first book to be published.

BlueRose

INR-000/-
FICTION

CHAPTER ONE
AN ACT OF MURDER?

It had been over a year since I had opened my own detective agency. I had given it, what I thought, a very sophisticated name – STAR DETECTIVE AGENCY. I would motivate the team by telling them that we were stars. I had not checked if there were any other detective agencies by that name and when STAR DETECTIVES PRIVATE LTD was registered, there were no objections from any quarter and my lawyer went ahead and registered it. A background as to why I decided to form this agency. I grew up in a family of achievers but somehow was never one for keeping my nose to the grindstone. For some reason, Sherlock Holmes fascinated me since I was a small kid and by the time I was sixteen, I had read his books about a hundred times. Had I read my school textbooks with this interest and ardour; I would have also been an achiever. I finished school and college with a reasonable amount of ease. I did not do exceptionally well, but then, I did not do exceptionally badly either. To satisfy the family I did my Chartered Accountancy and when I finished, I joined a multinational company in Bangalore selling tea. I could not stomach my boss, nor did I love my job. The only thing noteworthy in my fifteen months of stay was a forgery case that I cracked. Well to be fair, I had my share of luck.

It was my fifth month at the job when one of the staff got a voucher for me to approve. The amount was small, a sum of Rupees two hundred and fifty. However, it was for a strip of tablets and to me it seemed a bit too costly. I had always trusted my hunches especially when I felt uncomfortable and instead of signing the voucher, sent it to internal audit. They checked with the pharmaceutical shop and found that the cost was only Rupees twenty-five and someone had added a zero. Most of the time the person preparing the bill rarely has the time to write it in words. In this day and age, when computers are running our lives, a manually written bill was a rarity. A few, very few, did still come our way. The staff who submitted the voucher was hauled up and he claimed that he was innocent. A handwriting expert was called. The expert went on record stating that the staff who had submitted the voucher was innocent. The suspicion then fell on the cashier. Since I had been the one who had ignited this bomb, I was asked to be part of the investigative team and we went through all the vouchers of the last one year. It literally was like opening a Pandora's box and the cashier along with a few of the accounts staff had forged the vouchers, manipulated the accounts and stolen a fair bit of money. Some of the bank records had been forged using blank bank letterheads. The auditors too had been careless. I loved this assignment and for more than six months was in some sort of a world where I imagined I was Sherlock Holmes. I had a colleague from internal audit by the name of Gautam Mitra who was truly a big help. Since the accounts were partly computerised, on the IT side, I got help from a pretty IIT Bombay engineering graduate called Jayanthi Natarajan. Jayanthi was a big help and highly intelligent. In about six months, I could figure out approximately when the fraud had started. I submitted my report, pointed out the checks and balances that were absent and suggested how such a fraud could be avoided in future.

The management of the company was impressed and notwithstanding the poor picture painted of me by my boss, they offered to promote me and make me the number two man in Internal Audit. The tiger had now tasted blood and I had decided that I was going to devote my life to solving crimes and these corporate jobs were much too mundane. In this time, however, two developments had taken place. I had fallen in love with Jayanthi but had too much of an inferiority complex to tell her that; and Gautam and myself had become close friends.

Luckily for me, this forgery case got me in touch with the police and I came across an energetic guy by the name of Pramod Pandey, who was going to retire in a month from the detective force. Suddenly the thought struck me that why not start my detective agency and after a long chat over lunch with Pramod, I decided to take a dive and we started the STAR DETECTIVE AGENCY. I discussed this with Gautam and was wondering what his reaction would be. Gautam, at first, could not believe his ears and thought that I was doing a stupid thing by throwing away a good job. When I explained to him that it was not possible for me now to sit and warm the seat of my pants on a mundane nine to five job, he saw light. His next words were music to my ears, as he asked, "Prakash, is there a vacancy in your new firm for someone like me?" I jumped out of the chair and gave him a big hug and said, "Gautam, if you also join Star Detective Agency, we will all be stars!"

That was the first time I used this line and it worked like magic. The best part was that both Pramod and Gautam had not even once asked me about salaries and my potential clients. Now I was hoping I could get Jayanthi also to join us and in the afternoon when we were discussing some print outs that she had taken for me, I told her that I was planning to quit and start a detective agency. Jayanthi was taken aback and asked me if I had asked my parents. I told her very frankly that my parents would never approve and asking their permission was like asking for the moon. She hid a smile and then said, "Prakash, nowadays, to run a detective agency, you need a good Information Technology resource. I have done a course in forensic technology and ethical hacking. I found the courses fascinating and truly I have enjoyed this short investigation that we have done together. Can I join your agency as the Information Technology head?"

Modesty, years of upbringing and being the typical shy guy who was not very articulate with the gentler sex, prevented me from hugging her the way I had hugged Gautam. I was tongue tied for a few minutes and Jayanthi probably seeing the admiration and happiness on my face blushed a bit and put her head down to avert my admiring gaze.

"Jayanthi, you are immediately appointed as Chief Technology Officer of Star Detective Agency and very soon we will all be stars."

I now had my team in place. I had to have my finances in place too and I had not done my homework too well as to the finances I would require. Anyway, the first thing I did after speaking to Jayanthi was call my brother who was a big shot in an organization of repute. I told him of my plans. He tried his best to dissuade me from doing such a stupid thing. I, of course, told him, nothing doing, I had my team in place and we were all set. Bangalore was now an exciting city, the Silicon Valley of the East. I was very sure that it would grow to be one of the most happening cities in India. It was no longer the sleepy pensioner's paradise that it once was. Against his better sense, and before I knew, he and my sister-in-law had promised me the princely sum of Rupees thirty lakhs. In one hour, I got a phone call from my parents who too tried their best to dissuade me from embarking on this crazy venture. When they saw that I was adamant, my mom and dad committed another thirty lakhs and STAR DETECTIVE AGENCY was truly on its way.

I called for a meeting at my favourite joint, Koshy's, which is a comfortable restaurant located at St Marks Road, close to our office. Koshy's has the Raj interior, which reminds one of the days when India was a colony. All four of us were present, Jayanthi, Gautam, Pramod and I. I first thanked each one of them for joining me and said that we were equal partners in this venture. I mentioned that my parents and brother had committed a sum of Rupees sixty lakhs. I was hoping that this would see us through the initial days, and that once our notice period was up, we could move into our new premises. I told them frankly that as of date I did not know where our new premises would be situated. Jayanthi then mentioned that we could use her Dad's garage and a room on top of the garage for free. As of now it was empty, and it was at a fairly central place called Malleshwaram. The rest of the gang including me clapped and I was amazed at the speed things were falling in place. Gautam and Pramod not to be left behind assured me that they would not ask for salaries till such time that things stabilized. They had savings which would tide them over for three months. Jayanthi too chipped in and said the same condition held for her. I, of course, even though I had no savings stated that I too would manage. I had a sneaky idea that I would use the room on top of the garage as a place to stay. Pramod had his own house in Bangalore reasonably close to Malleshwaram. Gautam, who was a bachelor like me, was staying in a rented flat on Convent Road and reiterated that he could manage for three months on his own.

After three months, our notice period completed, the three of us moved into our new office. The garage was the place we would see our clients in, and the room on the top was where we would brainstorm and where we would each have our own cubicle. Jayanthi's parents had agreed to allow me to stay in the room on top of the garage till such time that I got rooms elsewhere. They were not too happy about it and were probably hoping that my connection with Jayanthi would only be on the professional front. They were not very impressed with a guy who was opening a Detective agency. I did not know what plans Jayanthi had, but in a matter of days, breakfast came for me from their house. Invariably lunch would be given to us in the office and often Gautam and I had dinner in Jayanthi's house. Jayanthi had purchased computers and other equipment which would enable her to exploit the technology available. We were completely ready to accept clients.

Our first client, Mr Gowda, came through Pramod. This gentleman's eighteen-year-old daughter disappeared one morning from her house and coincidentally their neighbour's son had also vanished. The gentleman whose name was Mr S.R. Gowda was a little distraught and so was his neighbour one Mr Mirchandani. Mr Gowda had come to Pramod through a contact and wanted this to be very discreet. Both Mr Mirchandani and Mr Gowda were upset and a little incoherent. I requested Pramod and Jayanthi to handle this case. There were certain tricks of the trade which we had to learn from Pramod. All said and done, nothing can beat experience. But in the same breath, if the environment changes, then the experience of earlier years is reduced to naught. To give an example that is relevant to today's time, you may be the best horse cart driver in the world, but nobody will hire you. Far better to be an average driver of cars. Pramod's experience and Jayanthi's new skills would make an unbeatable combination. The first thing Pramod asked from the two neighbours was who their kids' best friends were. The fathers gave them a list of names and Pramod and Jayanthi went to have a chat with these kids. After speaking to all their friends individually and explaining to them how these kids could be in danger being all alone and how they were too young to elope etc, we got our first break. One of the kids had received a message from Mr Gowda's daughter. It had an attachment of a picture showing these two by the side of the river with a nice hotel in the background. Pramod immediately asked the two parents to check if any money was missing at home. They got back very fast that about Rupees three thousand was missing from both houses. Jayanthi got the message and picture forwarded to her. As Jayanthi rushed to her desk, she explained to me that since the picture was digital, meaning taken through a digital camera or mobile, she had technology that could get the location. Jayanthi came down in five minutes and we had the spot where the picture was taken. Talk about lucky breaks. The good news was conveyed to the two dads and they were told to lose no time in getting down to the hotel which was approximately two hundred kilometres from Bangalore. There Pramod advised the dads to carry the photographs of the two kids and told them not to be too harsh. In fact, Pramod advised them that if the kids wanted, the dads should agree to get them married. The more disapproval they show, the more likely the kids would run away again. The next day we got a call from the fathers saying the runaways were safe home and the dads had agreed to get them married once they completed their education. They could not thank us enough and we were happy that the first case was cracked so fast. The key here was that we had spoken to the kids' friends and Jayanthi's knowledge of forensics helped us. This truly was a lucky break for us, and we celebrated making out our first invoice to Mr Gowda for the princely sum of Rupees ten thousand. He was impressed, and I was smart enough to pretend that this had taken a great deal of effort and work.

The next case was one relating to a missing cashier. The cashier cum accountant of a small factory manufacturing basic auto-spares had not been coming to work for the past three days. The proprietor was unable to get in touch with him. His family also was anxious as he had not come home for four nights and had reported him missing at the local police station. I immediately asked Gautam to take care of this and requested him to keep me in the loop. I asked Pramod to accompany Gautam. We were all smart enough to know that if we could learn from and use Pramod's experience, combine our brains and technology we would be on a winning trajectory. Pramod asked Gautam to examine the cash book first. Gautam examined the cash book and saw that as per the book a substantial sum had been deposited in the bank. However, when Pramod and Gautam examined the statements sent by the bank for the same period, there was no sign of the money deposited there. The money that was supposed to be deposited in the bank had probably found its way into the cashier's pocket. Pramod explained to the proprietor, who had hired us, that this was a fraud. As this was a case of robbery, the proprietor should file a case with the police. Pramod would help the proprietor file the case. The proprietor wanted to know if we could help locate the cashier. Pramod agreed but said that this would cost more. The proprietor readily agreed. Pramod explained to the proprietor that if at all, by some bad luck, the cashier was killed or met with an accident, the fact that the proprietor did not report this embezzlement may go against the proprietor. After having registered a complaint with the police, Pramod and Gautam came back to the office and we discussed the case. Pramod mentioned that in most cases the cashier goes missing because of one of these reasons: a woman is involved, or he has lost money due to gambling, or he is an alcoholic, or has a drug problem. Pramod mentioned that since the cashier was missing from home it was likely that either a woman was involved, or he was gambling and had incurred a huge debt.

Immediately after the meeting, Pramod, Gautam and I visited the house of the cashier. It was a small neat house in a place called Sahakar Nagar tucked away in the north of Bangalore. After speaking to his distraught wife, we found that the cashier was a person of regular habits. Left the house at the same time and came home exactly at the same time. Pramod wanted to look at his cupboard and when he saw the small room that the cashier and his wife shared, he had second thoughts. The room was sparklingly clean and so was the cupboard. The shirts, underwear and other garments had been arranged so neatly that it was impossible to think of the cashier as a thief. They had two school going kids. Pramod enquired if they had any financial problems. The wife admitted that they were not very well off financially, but they were able to make two ends meet. Pramod enquired if there had ever been any delay in paying the school fees. The wife replied that the school fees had always been paid on time. We left the house soon after and had a brief discussion over a cup of tea at a nearby restaurant. Pramod had changed his opinion on what could have happened. Either the cashier had been kidnapped and then killed while on his way to the bank to deposit the money or he had met with an accident. Pramod made out a route chart from the office to the cashier's house and saw that there were four police stations and six hospitals. We rushed back to the cashier's house and got a recent photograph of the cashier which we took with us. We hired an autorickshaw and started checking the hospitals and police stations on the way. At the third police station, we struck gold. An accident had taken place in the previous week at a crossing. A bus had collided with a scooter on which there were two male individuals. The driver of the scooter had died instantaneously, and the pillion rider had suffered a head injury and was in a coma and had been kept in a ward at the Government hospital. Pramod used his influence as an ex policeman and requested that he see the scooter. One policeman escorted the three of us into a yard outside and showed us where the scooter was placed. Though the scooter was a wreck, the front of the scooter which had a space for storage below the handles was not badly damaged with the cover only slightly dented. Pramod waited till we were alone and drew out a small pen knife from his pocket. He drew out the blade and after applying some pressure opened the storage space. There was a cloth bag which was tied with a string and when Pramod opened it we could see the stash of currency notes. Pramod took the bag, asked for the address of the hospital and we left after thanking the cops at the police station.

We reached the cashier's factory and were lucky that the proprietor was still there. We submitted a verbal report and Gautam, after checking with the cash book, found that the cash exactly tallied with the amount that was to be banked. Pramod explained to the proprietor that the cashier had met with an accident while on his way to deposit the money. We took the proprietor along and went to the hospital. We found that the cashier had suffered a head injury and was in a coma. We were informed that if the patient was lucky, then the patient will survive if the blood clot in the brain dissolves. The proprietor said that he would try to get the cashier moved to a hospital with better facilities and Pramod then left us to help the police stations join all the dots. Three reports had been made, the first by the cashier's wife that the cashier was missing, the second by the proprietor that the money was stolen and the third at the police station where the accident was reported. Pramod also wanted to check if the family of the driver of the scooter had been notified.

We celebrated the second successful closure and we were learning. We had to have an open mind and start off with a premise. However, we had to be ready, depending on the facts, to change our mind. There was logic in investigating and, so far, we had been lucky with the two cases. We invoiced the proprietor the sum of twenty thousand rupees. We also decided that if we got more cases, we had to buy a couple of cars.

The number of cases we received started to multiply. Cash frauds, runaway couples, keeping a watch on the spouse or fiancé, investigating the background of prospective spouses, computer frauds on the lines of giving money to a person one has become friendly online. As the social dating sites and chat sites increased, cases of blackmail also started to increase. All of us were working almost twelve to fourteen hours per day. There were many occasions when we worked all seven days a week.

It was after six months, that we got our first murder case. Thanks to the second case where we had tracked down the missing cashier and coupled with the fact that we went out of our way to help the local authorities, we had built a good rapport with the police. There were times when the detectives were preoccupied with several cases and would give us a case to sort out, with the line of investigation we should approach. This was the first such case. It was rather grisly and at the time the case was handed over to us, the detectives of the department were simultaneously investigating three murder cases that had created headlines. Somewhere between Mysore and Bangalore, along the Kaveri river, a suitcase had floated to the banks and it had a headless torso. Obviously, the perpetrators of the crime had not expected that the suitcase would float up as it had been weighed down with stones. What had happened was the heavy monsoons had increased the flow of the river and the silt at the bottom had been stirred. This made the suitcase tilt and the water had weakened the fabric of the suitcase, so the stones had fallen out. This had allowed the suitcase to float up with the decomposed torso. The big break that the police had got was that the victim was wearing a tailored shirt and a photo of the tailor label had been given to us. A photo of the shirt too had been given to us. What the detectives wanted us to do was to trace out the tailor, and see from there, if we could get information on the victim. This was fairly straight forward and Pramod and Gautam were given this investigation. There was no money in this, but the experience would be great for all of us. The first break itself was a learning experience, as to how, even in a seemingly hopeless case, vital clues could be gathered. This would also improve our rapport with the authorities further, assuming we cracked this case. The forensic details were that the torso was of a male individual aged around thirty-five years and he had been stabbed in the heart while drugged or asleep. The label of the tailor was 'Seetharaman's'. Gautam and Pramod agreed that the best way to start was to visit a tailor and find out how the tailor got these labels. On checking with the neighbourhood tailor, we found that the labels are made out by a fabricator and there were several fabricators at the city market in Bangalore. The first fabricator we went to, told us after seeing the photograph that it looked as if this label had been made in Mysore. There were only two such fabricators in Mysore and he could check up with us right now if we wished over the telephone. On checking up with the second, the reply was that this label had been fabricated by them for a tailor in Mysore. Pramod and Gautam immediately left for Mysore. There in Mysore, after meeting the fabricator and getting the address of the tailor, the team visited the tailor. The tailor had his shop in an upmarket area of Mysore called Jayalakshmipuram. There the tailor's assistant helped us go through his order book. In the order book, the tailor cuts a small piece of the fabric and staples it in the order book against the relevant order number. We found three orders that matched with the photograph of the shirt that we had been given by the detectives. Thankfully all the three lived close by and Pramod along with Gautam paid each of them a visit. The first two were very much alive and kicking and we all thought that probably we would be hitting a dead end if the third was also alive and kicking.

When we reached the third address, Pramod and Gautam were impressed by the house. It was an independent house, not too big but reasonably spacious and with a nice front lawn. When we rang the bell, an elderly lady opened the house. When we enquired about Parthasarathy Kumar, the person who had ordered this shirt to be tailored, the lady asked Pramod and Gautam to step in.

The lady wanted to know the purpose of this visit. Gautam told her that there was a possibility that this Parthasarathy Kumar could have been murdered. The lady was close to tears and told them that Parthasarathy Kumar was her younger brother. He was based in Bangalore and his wife had said that he had left for Canada about six months back. According to his wife, Kumar had a mistress in Canada and had deserted her for his mistress. The lady mentioned that they came from a very conservative family and this was a big shock for the entire family. To the best of her knowledge her younger brother was not one to do such a thing. Pramod and Gautam then went on to explain how it was important that they speak to Kumar's wife and asked the lady to give them the address of Kumar's house in Bangalore. Pramod also requested for a recent photograph of Kumar. The lady was only too happy to oblige, and after giving the two of them some steaming hot coffee, made Pramod promise her that he would let her know what exactly happened to her brother. Pramod and Gautam made their way back to Bangalore. Pramod decided that the next step was to find out if Parthasarathy Kumar had a passport and if so, was it used to go to Canada?

Pramod made use of his contacts and with the help of the Bangalore address, Mysore address and the photograph traced the passport number of Parthasarathy Kumar. The last time it had been used, was to enter Bangalore, India from Toronto roughly ten months back. After that it had not been used for leaving India, as per the immigration records. Armed with this knowledge Pramod and Gautam decided to visit his wife who lived in a place called Wilson Gardens in Bangalore. Pramod wanted to do a background check on Kumar to find out more about this person.

The background check revealed that Parthasarathy owned an export-import firm. This was run by three directors, two of them based in India and one based in Canada. The firm was doing well and in the last financial year had done a total turnover of USD fifty million. The firm had made a tidy profit of over USD four million. Parthasarathy Kumar was the major shareholder. He held fifty two percent of the shareholding and the balance was held by the other two partners. Pramod used his contacts and found an employee working in the firm, which was called Maple and Peepul Exports Imports Private Ltd. The name of the employee was Rajesh Bharat and he worked there as the Marketing Manager. Pramod found out the inner workings from Rajesh. The firm was a trading firm and exported agriproducts and agricultural machinery. The firm also imported the same. The bulk of the imports were grain harvesters used in Punjab. Parthasarathy was a very upright boss and the rumour was he had flown to Canada to broker a big business deal. Nothing had been heard from him so far. There were talks of a woman being involved but Rajesh who had interacted with Parthasarathy a lot, did not believe this. He was unable to get along with the other Director based here and was planning to resign.

Armed with this information Gautam and Pramod made a visit to Parthasarathy's wife. The house in Wilson Gardens was an independent house and had a neat, manicured lawn in front. The door was opened by Parthasarathy's wife herself and they introduced themselves as employees of Star Detective Agency. They mentioned that they had been assigned to trace her husband by a creditor who had to receive a lot of money from Parthasarathy. This money had been lent in a personal capacity. Did she have any idea about the whereabouts of Parthasarathy?

The wife, whose name was Meenakshi, burst into tears. One day seven months back, the company driver had returned from office and had requested her to pack a bag for Parthasarathy mentioning that an urgent trip had come up and he had to go to Canada. The driver said Parthasarathy would call her from office or on reaching Canada. So far, no news had been received. The other director whose name was Kalyana Raman, had told her about six months back, that there were strong rumours that Parthasarathy was involved with a woman in Toronto. The office had also received no news from Parthasarathy ever since he had landed in Toronto. Gautam and Pramod comforted her and said that this was unlikely. She could help and give the two of them the toothbrush and razor that was used by her husband. This would help them find out what exactly had happened to her husband. They also cautioned her that their visit and the fact that she had given them the toothbrush and razor should be kept a total secret.

On their return to the office, Pramod mentioned that he would try to get a DNA profiling done of Parthasarathy either through the dried saliva on the brush or through a hair that remained on the razor. We would then try to match the DNA with that of the torso. This torso seemed now to be that of Parthasarathy, and the needle of suspicion seemed to be pointing to the other director.

We got the news after two days that the DNA proofing was a success and indeed the torso was that of the late Parthasarathy Kumar. Armed with all this information and with a detailed report, Pramod and Gautam made a visit to the detective who had assigned us this case. I got a call from the dealing Inspector congratulating us on the excellent job done by our team and on bringing the case so far. The next week we got the information that the other director had got Parthasarathy murdered and had hatched this conspiracy. The main reason was that Parthasarathy had caught him embezzling money by over invoicing suppliers. Kalyana Raman had speculated heavily in the share market and lost crores of rupees. He led a lavish lifestyle and could not sustain this anymore without further money. Parthasarathy had asked him to resign in a fortnight or face exposure. Kalyana Raman had paid some hit men to kill Parthasarathy and planted a rumour that Parthasarathy was leading another life in Toronto. The police completed the investigation and made their arrests. It made sensational news for a couple of days in this part of the world and for us is it was a big learning experience. Gautam, Pramod, Jayanthi and I worked backwards and tried to see how we could have cracked the case had there been no tailor-made shirt and the only clue available was a readymade shirt. The other learning was how DNA profiling can be used to construct an identity. This science has progressed a lot. In earlier times, the only way was to circulate the likely description of the victim and the approximate period the victim was missing and pray that somebody replied to the circular.

Now that we were in this business, the three of us, Jayanthi, Gautam and I took lessons in handling of firearms. We also took a course in basic self-defence and hired a retired RAW agent to give us lessons on how to follow someone. It had now been one year since the STAR DETECTIVE AGENCY had been formed and it was thriving. The four of us were now finding ourselves submerged in work and wondered if we should hire a couple of extra hands. All four of us were now making more money than we had before. I was grateful to Pramod for his guidance and contacts with the police.

Suddenly, we found ourselves in the middle of a big murder case. One day in October, the newspapers carried some sensational headlines. It had very briefly been reported on television, the night before. Bishal Dev Bandhopadhya, one of the successful entrepreneurs of today's generation had been poisoned. The office boy who had prepared his coffee in the morning had been taken into custody. The details were as follows. Bishal, a successful entrepreneur in the field of vaccines had arrived at work around eight in the morning in his posh office, located at Richmond Circle. As was his routine, he had his morning cup of coffee. After three and a half hours or so, he was found collapsed on his table and was rushed to a nearby private hospital, where he was declared dead on arrival. The post-mortem reports were awaited. The half empty cup of coffee in the office of Bishal contained traces of rat-poison. The news of Bishal's death had a noticeably big impact on the share price of International Vaccines, the company managed by Bishal.

I returned to the office from some routine investigations on an embezzlement and found two visitors waiting for me. As soon as I settled in, Gautam came with the two ladies to see me. The first lady was introduced to me as the cashier's wife. This was the cashier mentioned earlier who had met with an accident while on his way to the bank to deposit money. The second was simply introduced as her friend. I requested Jayanthi also to join in as these ladies would be more comfortable with a lady around. Pramod was out on a case so it would only be the three of us. Before we could start, the friend of the cashier's wife broke down and started crying. Jayanthi and the cashier's wife started to comfort her. The conversation was mainly in Kannada, the local language. Finally, the cashier's wife spoke up and mentioned that her friend was the wife of the office boy in Bishal's office. The office boy had been taken into custody and was the prime suspect in the murder case. The family had thought that he would be released soon but apparently it looked like he would be jailed for a long period of time. The office boy was innocent, and his wife had got to know from the cashier's wife about how we had traced the cashier when he had gone missing. The wife of the office boy then took out a small cloth bag and handed it over to Jayanthi. When Jayanthi opened it, we saw that it was full of jewellery. The lady mentioned that they had no money, and this was the fees that the family could give us to investigate this murder and prove that her husband, the office boy was innocent. Jayanthi returned the bag and told her that we would investigate the murder and we would discuss the fees later. After assuring the two ladies that we would take up this case, Jayanthi comforted the office boy's wife saying that if the office boy were innocent, we would prove this to the world. I was taken aback by the way our reputation was spreading and was a little touched by the way the office boy's wife was ready to give all the jewellery to us. Very soon Pramod returned and I briefed him of the developments and Pramod then mentioned that he would have a chat at the station handling the case. Pramod returned in the evening with the good news that we could be involved in the case right from the beginning. The police were ready to share their findings and we in turn should also share our observations. They would put a junior detective on the case and as far as interrogation went, all of us would be present.

There was however one condition, there would be no interaction with the press from our side. All dealings with the press would be by the police. We would also have to file a statement with the police that our firm had been hired by the office boy to investigate the case. Once these formalities were completed, we could start the investigation, which would be in a day's time. The office of Bishal had been sealed and the half-finished cup of coffee had been sent for analysis. We got busy with the documentation from our end where we got the office boy's wife to formally appoint us and give us a power of attorney to act on her behalf in all matters relating to the investigation of the murder. During the day Pramod informed us that the coffee from the cup had been analysed and it was full of strychnine, a powerful rat poison. The police on sending a team of two detectives to the office of Bishal had located a box, labelled 'POISON', in the pantry. Those contents too would be analysed, and things were not looking too good for the office boy.

The next day began with Gautam and me, along with the police detective, visiting Bishal's office at nine in the morning. Prior to this, I had requested Jayanthi and Pramod to find out as much as possible about Bishal and his organization. I had no plan of investigation lined up as such and was playing it totally by the ear. The office was indeed a posh one. This was the corporate office. They had one factory in a place called Hosur, on the Karnataka – Tamil Nadu border, and a second in Electronic City in Bangalore. The office was of a rectangular shape. The breadth of one rectangle had Bishal's personal office and the room of his associate. On the other breadth was the kitchen and the reception. The length of the rectangle was an open plan office which also housed the toilets, conference room, the printer, and the fax room. There was plenty of ventilation and light making the office a pleasant place to work in. The colour was blue and white and in all, the interior decoration of the office gave a good ambience. We had left instructions that we wanted to meet all the employees of the organization working in this office and anyone else who had been there before Bishal had been rushed to the hospital.

When Gautam, Kamal (the police detective) and I entered the office we were told by the receptionist, a lady by the name of Usha, that all the employees had assembled in the conference room and were waiting for us. As we entered the conference room, there was a buzz of conversation which immediately stopped when we entered the room. The first thing that struck me was that the employees were looking quite cheerful, and as much as I tried, I could not see even one sad face. The employees were looking very relaxed. I had not seen them before Bishal's murder, but one did not have to be a Sherlock Holmes to conclude that Bishal was a boss who was not liked. There was a slight tension in the air and in all probability, it was there because of us. I scanned all the faces before me and at least prima-facie nobody looked guilty or scared.

We took our seats at the head of the table and Kamal asked me to give a brief talk as to why we were there. I took a deep breath and tried to give a speech that I thought would help break the ice.

"Good morning, ladies and gentlemen. At the outset, my sincere apologies for asking you all to assemble here this morning. This is because of the tragic and untimely death of your boss, Mr Bishal Dev Bandhopadhya. I am here with Mr Kamal Prasad, a detective of the Bangalore Police force and with Mr Gautam Mitra, a private detective working for the Star Detective Agency. I am Prakash Chari, also working for the Star Detective Agency. We have been assigned to investigate the death of Mr Bishal. I would earnestly request for your cooperation and advise you to be frank with us when we meet each of you in private in this conference room. I promise you that we will try our best to close the initial part of our investigation in a maximum of a week or ten days. I am also leaving our contact numbers with all of you. Should anything strike you as having been out of place or having a bearing on the tragic demise of Mr Bishal, do share it with us, irrespective of the time of the day or night. However, before we break up, we would like all of you to introduce yourselves, one by one and share the following details: your name, your role in the organization, how long you have been in the organization and the organization you were working for prior to joining this one."

There was pin drop silence after I had spoken. Suddenly there was a palpable tension in the room. The nine employees present looked at one another and then avoided any sort of eye contact with me. Of the nine, four were ladies. The silence continued and I was forced to speak once again.

"Please, let us go clockwise from this gentleman", I said, and pointed to the person on my left.

The person on my left was a good looking individual, dressed very well and with a bearing that suggested that with Bishal, he also held a senior position. He got up from his seat and I signalled that he remains seated. He sat down and began to introduce himself.

"Good morning to you, Mr Chari and your team and to my team here. My name is Shantanu Gurusekhar. I am the only person remaining from the original team that started this venture. I am the Director, Research and Development. My time is divided between the works and the corporate office. Apart from Research and Development, I also oversee production and marketing. I began my career with this organization. Thank You".

So, my guess was right, this was the guy who was probably, next to Bishal in the hierarchy. Since Bishal and this character had worked almost together from the start of this organization, he would know a lot of the history of this company and would probably have played an important role in the recruitment of the team. I mentally filed the fact that this person should be the first person we should interrogate.

"Thank you, Mr Gurusekhar. The next person, please."

The lady sitting next to Mr Gurusekhar was a young thing. Probably in her mid-twenties. I guessed she would be an Executive Assistant of sorts and I was not very wrong.

"Good morning. My name is Devi Prabhakar. I work as Officer, Marketing. I deal with the marketing side of our vaccines. It has been six months since I started working here and before that I was working with Pfizer. It's been two years since I completed my post-graduation in molecular biology from the Johns Hopkins University in the USA."

"Thank you, Devi. Please can we continue with the next person?"

There was another lady sitting next to Devi. She looked to be in her mid-thirties and was dressed in a sari. From her bearing and looks I guessed she would have been Bishal's secretary.

"Good morning. My name is Mrs Seghal and I am holding the post of secretary to both Mr Bishal and Mr Gurusekhar. I have been working here for the past five months. Prior to this I was working in Bishop Cotton School for Girls."

Yes, from this lady we could get to know a lot about Bishal. She did not seem to be the type to gossip but again there was not a hint of sadness on anyone's face that Bishal was no more.

"Thank You Mrs Seghal."

There was an elderly gentleman sitting next to the lady. He was dressed in the old-fashioned style of a half-sleeves shirt not tucked in. He had a big red vermillion mark on his forehead. He seemed to have been chewing betel leaf and was feeling a little out of place in this gathering.

"Good morning, Sirs, my name is Hemantha Gowda. Sir, I deal with the Patents and Trademarks office and with the Health Ministry on all matters relating to introduction of new drugs. Prior to my joining here, I was the Chief Clerk in the office of the Patents and Trademarks. Sir, it has been two years since I have been employed here."

A file pusher and a person who had to deal with the bureaucracy. Probably had a lot of contacts at the lower level of the Patents and Trademarks office. This guy probably co-ordinated with the lawyers of this firm. Essentially his job was to see that files moved from one table to another. Mr Gowda would not know much of what happened in the office. Most of his time would be spent outdoors dealing with the bureaucracy.

The guy sitting next to Mr Gowda was a youngish chap. He seemed to be in his late thirties or early forties. My guess was that he was the CFO of this organization.

"Good morning. I am Mahesh Ramachandran. I work here as the CFO. I have been working here for the last two years. Prior to this I was with Hindustan Unilever."

I had to be a little careful here. Why leave such a good organization to join this company? Somehow things did not seem to make sense here. I was a little lost in thought when I heard the next person speak. She was a lady in her mid-thirties and before I could even gauge her, she said, "A very good morning. I am Neena Gupta. I am the Chief of HR and I have been here for three years. Prior to joining here, I was working with Hindustan Petroleum."

The lady sitting next to her spoke almost at once.

"Good morning, I am Usha Murthy. I work as the receptionist and have been here for slightly over a year. Prior to this I was working with Hindustan Machine Tools."

Again, before I could react, the next person said, "Good morning everyone, I am Rohit Soundarajan and I am the Chief of Legal. I have been working here for about four months. Prior to this I was working in a legal company called Mullah and Mullah."

The last guy spoke up and he was Suresh Sridhar and in charge of both office administration and Public Relations. He had worked here for three months and prior to this had been working in the public sector undertaking called BHEL. What struck me was that other than Gurusekhar, nobody had worked here for a long period of time. The office boy, the only other employee was not here. I just wanted to check if there was any other employee who worked here but was not present. I asked Gurusekhar for confirmation on this point and he replied in the affirmative. All the employees other than the office boy were present.

I concluded the meeting by thanking all those present. I requested that the employees go to their respective places and continue with their jobs. I would call each of them for a detailed discussion during the day. We would be here till six pm and would again request the presence of some of the employees tomorrow. All the employees filed out of the room and Kamal, Gautam and I were alone in the conference room. I asked the two of them if they sensed anything amiss and Gautam replied that no employee seemed to have stayed here long. I told Gautam that this was what struck me too. Kamal too had noticed that nobody seemed to be feeling too sad on Bishal's death. We decided that we would call the Chief of HR first and listen to what she had to say. But before that, I asked Kamal if he could share with us all the facts relating to Bishal's death that had come on record.

Kamal began to read out the facts and observations from the file. At around twelve noon, the police station located in Richmond Circle got a message from the Richmond Nursing Home that a high-profile individual by the name of Bishal Dev Bandhopadhya had been brought to the hospital in an unconscious state. Within a few minutes of arrival, he had breathed his last. The person was a male Indian of about thirty years of age and from both the pallor and description by the people who had brought him to the hospital, it seemed to be a case of severe food poisoning. The hospital wanted to know whether they could go ahead with the autopsy. The local police had immediately informed the incident of an unnatural death to the investigative wing of the police headquarters. The headquarters had summoned a few detectives to go to the office of Bishal Dev. There the detectives had found a half empty cup of coffee which they seized and sent to the forensic laboratory for testing. They had sealed the office of Bishal and told all the employees present that they should not leave the premises. The analysis of the coffee showed huge amount of strychnine in the coffee and when the detectives came back to the office, armed with this information, they found a tin in the kitchen labelled 'POISON'. They checked this with the office boy who mentioned that this was used to kill rats. After a preliminary interrogation, the detectives concluded that other than the office boy there could be nobody else who could have served coffee to Bishal. The office boy was taken into custody for interrogation. While searching Bishal's office room they also came across a small steel container on his table and on analysing the contents found that that too was rat poison. This led to a new line of thought that perhaps this could be a case of suicide. The body had been sent to a government hospital for the doctors to conduct an autopsy and determine the cause of death. This was what was on file.

www.ingramcontent.com/pod-product-compliance
Ingram Content Group UK Ltd.
Pitfield, Milton Keynes, MK11 3LW, UK
UKHW041945230426
12048UKWH00008B/148